THE DARE TO BE DIFFERENT BOOK

SEVEN DARES TO EMBRACE, ENHANCE AND EXPLOIT YOUR OWN UNIQUENESS

MAGNUS LINDKVIST

FOR OTHER TITLES
IN THE SERIES...

CONCISE ADVICE LAB

SMALL BOOKS: BIG IDEAS

CLEVER CONTENT, DYNAMIC IDEAS, PRACTICAL
SOLUTIONS AND ENGAGING VISUALS –
A CATALYST TO INSPIRE NEW WAYS OF THINKING
AND PROBLEM-SOLVING IN A COMPLEX WORLD

www.lidpublishing.com/product-category/concise-advice-series

To Roy
There are many like Roy
But nobody exactly like Roy

Published by
LID Publishing
An imprint of LID Business Media Ltd.
LABS House, 15-19 Bloomsbury Way,
London, WC1A 2TH, UK

info@lidpublishing.com
www.lidpublishing.com

A member of:

BPR ✸

businesspublishersroundtable.com

© Magnus Lindkvist, 2024
© LID Business Media Limited, 2024
Reprinted in 2024

Printed by Imak Ofset

ISBN: 978-1-915951-26-7
ISBN: 978-1-915951-27-4 (ebook)

Cover and page design: Caroline Li

THE DARE TO BE DIFFERENT BOOK

SEVEN DARES TO EMBRACE, ENHANCE AND EXPLOIT YOUR OWN UNIQUENESS

MAGNUS LINDKVIST

MADRID | MEXICO CITY | LONDON
BUENOS AIRES | BOGOTA | SHANGHAI

CONTENTS

"

How glorious
it is – and also
how painful – to
be an exception.

"

Alfred de Musset

INTRODUCTION
MAKING THE DIFFERENCE

You are different. That is not just a fact, it is a marvel of existence.

Your genes and the traits they express are unique. By 0.1%, on average, to be scientifically precise.[1] That may not sound like a lot, but the billions of tapestries woven from this decimal are infinite regarding eye colour variations, fingerprints or dislike of coriander.

Biochemically, you are one of a kind.

Furthermore, the combination of experiences and impressions you have had in your lifetime is even more unique. Every human life contains multitudes — intricate layers of experiences, beliefs, traumas and triumphs. No single human being has lived your exact life, and every day, the stream of thoughts, images and activities conspire to chisel out an even more unique version of you, like waves pounding cliffs on a shore into a different shape, slowly over many years. Experientially, you are singular.

You may be acutely aware of your uniqueness.

---

1 National Society of Genetic Counselors (2019). "Understanding genetic variation," American Society of Human Genetics. https://www.ashg.org/wp-content/uploads/2019/09/genetic-variation-essay.pdf

You may possess a particular talent or skill, in which case, being different might be a source of pride.

Or you may feel a sense of guilt and shame about yourself connected to your appearance, something you've experienced or an undefined sense of alienation. At those times, being different doesn't feel good — it makes you feel alone.

And there are countless situations where you will feel like part of a herd. Whether you're queuing up to go through airport security, waiting for a bus in the rain, or standing at a busy intersection full of pedestrians somewhere in the world. Here, you are just one of thousands going through your day and sharing not only the same space but also the same intention.

Sonder strikes — the name given to that dizzying recognition that every person around you lives a life as complex and emotionally turbulent as your own. A vertigo of sameness.

In these instances, you struggle to find even a tiny sliver of uniqueness in yourself.

Still, deep down lies your uniqueness, and this book is a celebration of that very quality.

It is a book about daring.

Dare to Be Different is a call to deepen, emphasize, express and sharpen what makes you distinct. Not just *being* different but seeing, thinking and doing differently.

WHY OUR UNIQUENESS MATTERS

Take a moment to search the web for images of 'Mount Everest, May 2019.' Hundreds of people had ended up in an eight-hour queue to reach the summit on that fateful day. What was once a unique adventure for Edmund Hillary and Sherpa Tenzing Norgay has become a pastime for the many.

You are different, but modern society has ways to make you adapt and fit in. Imagine a machine where the input is you, the unique individual described above, and the output is hordes of people who look, act and think the same. We are born original but risk dying as clones.

When you are young, you are on the outside looking in on the adult world. You often start by copying what they do. You try on your parents' clothes. You imitate what you see on TV or TikTok. You repeat things you have heard that resonate with you.

Schools teach us about the world, but their methods are based on copying. We copy to learn to write, we repeat facts given to us, and we duplicate what previous generations have done.

The specialization of the economy means that we don't sew our own clothes, dream up our own recipes, or build our own furniture anymore. We buy it at the closest supermarket or shopping mall, inadvertently becoming slaves to what others believe fashion, style or food should be like.

You go to great extents in the pursuit of feeling different. Just like advertising is a kind of tax on products that are not unique enough, the money we put in to have unique experiences is a kind of penalty.

Alarmingly often, you discover that thousands of others have the same unique idea as you. And on the very same day. Like, say, climbing Mount Everest.

You copy other people's dreams and wants without knowing. This is why vacation destinations are crowded, why there are bidding wars for places to live, and why more and more things look and feel like competitions – getting into a good university, getting a good job, living in a special place and so on.

The Digital Age has amplified this inclination. We often choose restaurants or tourist spots based on TripAdvisor's top 10 lists. Global bestseller charts guide our reading and listening choices. Streaming platforms suggest shows and movies based on the preferences of users similar to us. In the 21st century, copy/paste is intricately woven into our everyday decisions.

... MORE THAN EVER

The concept of the individual is a relatively modern creation. For millennia, we existed primarily as servants and slaves, our identities intertwined with the collective rather than standing alone. However, a few hundred years ago, the tides began to shift. Revolutionary ideas about freedom and personal rights started to crystallize.

From these ideas emerged the 'individual,' derived from a word meaning 'indivisible.' Suddenly, each person began to be seen as significant in their own right, independent of bloodlines, monarchs and deities.

In the last century, this notion has amplified dramatically. The individual's influence has expanded to an almost boundless extent.

Consider the Doomsday Curve, a chilling historical graph. It illustrates what percentage of the human population would be required to annihilate our global population entirely.

In our distant past, with only rudimentary weapons at our disposal, such a catastrophic event would have necessitated the involvement of every living person. It's a grim thought: a worldwide, fatal conflict followed by a solitary act of suicide to complete the extinction.

As time marched on and technology evolved, the tools of war grew more sophisticated — from crossbows to tanks. Now, fast forward to today. The Doomsday Curve shows a terrifying reduction in numbers. Just a handful of individuals, if they possess the right technological means, could unleash a pandemic or hijack the control systems of a nuclear arsenal.

We find ourselves in an era where fewer people than ever have the potential to inflict catastrophic harm on the rest of humankind. The power vested in the individual today is almost divine — an omnipotence that was once the stuff of myths is now a tangible reality.

And yet, we are increasingly asking whether humans will be needed in the coming century.

Goldman Sachs, a global bank, has estimated that more than 300 million jobs in the world may be automated into oblivion thanks to the emergence of artificial intelligence (AI). That is just below all the people employed in Europe and the US combined. Machines have always helped humans perform new tasks — from diggers enabling us to displace tons of dirt without the need for biceps to electron microscopes enabling doctors to explore new spaces in the human body. The worry about machines replacing humans is not new, but it may be merited this time.

AI has beaten human champions in chess (1997), *Jeopardy!* (2011), the Asian board game Go (2016), poker (2017) and StarCraft 2, a popular online strategy game (2019).

Furthermore, AI can predict protein structures in milliseconds, not the months and years it takes humans. ChatGPT, a user-friendly online tool that can generate answers and ideas to our questions, has, in a short period of time, become the world's favourite cowriter, research assistant and serial plagiarizer. Goldman Sachs's calculation of lost jobs might actually be a conservative estimate.

If machines are becoming better at previously unique human endeavours, what do humans need to become better at? How are we different from AI? What can only you do?

Being able to come up with good answers to these questions will only become more pronounced in the coming decades as AI continues to make inroads into our working lives.

THE GRETCHEN QUESTION

The Germans, of course, have a name for it: *gretchenfrage (Gretchen Question.)* Originally from Goethe's *Faust*, it denotes a direct question that seeks to unveil the honest thoughts and attitudes of the person questioned. The answer is often uncomfortable.

The Gretchen Question this book wants to pose is this: Do you want to compete, or do you want to create?

We usually bypass this question by making the activities one and the same. We compete in art or music and use tired clichés like 'innovate to find a competitive advantage.' The fact that both words – compete and create – begin with the same letter makes them sound alike.

But they are at opposite ends of the spectrum.

Competition is about fitting in. Its Latin origin — *com petare* — means to strive together. The first prerequisite in any competition is other competitors, and if you outperform them, you win. In sports, you win a gold medal. In business, you win market share, money and accolades.

Creation is about bringing something new into this world: a song, a work of art, a thought or a way of doing things. If done well, creation tends to make enemies, not awards.

Take the following famous example.

Ignaz Semmelweis, the 19th-century Hungarian physician, dramatically improved maternal health with his advocacy for hand hygiene in medical settings. At a Viennese hospital, he discovered that simply washing your hands could significantly reduce the incidence of puerperal fever among postpartum women. Yet, his potentially revolutionary findings were met with derision and disbelief by his contemporaries in the medical field.

Ostracized by the medical community and beset by a series of professional setbacks, Semmelweis became increasingly isolated. His frustration with the rejection of his findings manifested in his writings, which took on an urgent, almost pleading tone, straying from the dispassionate norms of scientific communication.

Ultimately, his continued advocacy and resultant stress took a severe toll on his mental health, culminating in a tragic end within the confines of a Viennese asylum. His story poses a profound dilemma:

Would you choose to compete, potentially reaping monetary rewards and accolades? Or would you opt to innovate and create despite the risk of misunderstanding and marginalization that may follow? This question encapsulates the stark reality faced by those who dare to disrupt established norms and practices.

This is a Gretchen Question.

THE GOAL OF THIS BOOK

You are most likely reading this alone somewhere in the world, either on a digital device or on paper. You may think of this as a solitary activity; you, a book, and perhaps a cup of coffee or a glass of Sauvignon Blanc. Nothing could be further from the truth. The device or book you are using is the result of dozens of companies collaborating, supplying pulp to paper mills or silicon chips to factories. The coffee or wine has an equally daunting list of supply chain nodes bringing beans to roasters or glass bottles to and from wineries. Autonomy is an illusion. Solitude too. No human is an island, but an archipelago floating in a vast ocean of interdependence.

Being different is, by definition, a social activity. What is your relationship to other archipelagoes? How do you differ and why? How can you embrace, enhance and exploit these differences? These are the questions underpinning this book.

Social media posts and business bestseller lists are full of success manuals in the 21st century. Usually featuring shortcuts or trite advice like 'find your passion.'

This book is not a success manual. It will not prescribe some universal 'secret' recipe to exploit your differences to make billions and retire early. As later sections will show, being different is a source of pain, not pleasure.

Another unfortunate feature of 21st-century societies is that we have mistaken identity for skill, controversy for insight, and equated accomplishment with money and fame. Your gender and skin colour may seem different, but they are also out of your control and constitute little use to other people. Stirring up controversy takes some courage but little effort. If you are seeking to dramatize some injustice, real or perceived, based on these accidental physical attributes, this book is not for you. The *Dare to Be Different Book* will dig deeper than identity politics and show how to handle misfortune more effectively than angry social media rants.

What this book aims to do is supply a scarce resource: meaning.

Modernity's conveniences, from streaming music to fast food, have made life easier but less meaningful. The effort behind buying a vinyl record or cooking from scratch gave us a sense of purpose that swiping on an app or a McDonald's meal lacks. Our ancestors had predefined paths, providing a clear sense of meaning. Today, we're free to forge our own, which is both liberating and daunting. Meaning is a personal exploration, found in actions big and small. Understanding our uniqueness is the starting point to finding deeper, individualized meaning in life.

The philosopher Søren Kierkegaard explained that anxiety is the dizzying effect of freedom, of paralyzing possibility, of the boundlessness of one's own existence.

If this book will lower this anxiety for you, make freedom less dizzying and provide a sense of meaning, it will have accomplished its goal.

HOW TO READ THIS BOOK

The Princeton psychologist George Miller had a fascinating insight in the mid-1950s. One that would lay the foundation for all modern phone numbers. He presented the insight in a paper called "The Magical Number Seven, Plus or Minus Two: Some Limits on Our Capacity for Processing Information." The title says it all: Humans have a special relationship with the number seven. This extends beyond cognitive barriers. The number of days a week, the number of colours in the rainbow, the seven deadly sins, the Seven Samurai, Snow White's seven dwarves, and the seven Chronicles of Narnia. Rome itself, it is believed, is built on seven hills.

Seven is a useful and inherently familiar structure to base this book on. Seven Ways — Seven Dares — to be different is not intended to be an exhaustive list or one based on a deep scientific insight but a playful wink to the long tradition of magical, magnificent sevens.

Part One: The first dare is to dig deep, far beyond the obvious. 'Dare to be different' risks sounding like a cheap marketing slogan wherein cool body piercings or hair dye are urged. The first dare will help us understand how and where to dig to find deep differences, not marketing gimmicks.

Part Two: The second dare is to be an outsider. Getting invited to parties is nice, but being different is about the benefits of distancing yourself from the crowd and thereby sacrificing party invitations, at least in the short run.

Part Three: The third dare is about accepting, sometimes even embracing, suffering. No one goes through this life unscathed, and even though we are biologically preconditioned to avoid discomfort, there lies value beyond the pain, like the gold hiding in a dragon's den.

Part Four: The fourth dare is particularly challenging in these individualistic times; being kind. We pay lip service to generosity and kindheartedness but often succumb to selfishness. A book about finding personal uniqueness could easily have slid into tired identity politics featuring the usual suspects of victimhood and vengeance. Being different is a social endeavour and you will need many people on your side. The key is kindness.

Part Five: The fifth dare is to move. The world is full of beauty, but not all of it is in the right place. To use the famous quote (most likely misattributed to Albert Einstein): "Everybody is a genius. But if you judge a fish by its ability to climb a tree, it will live its whole life believing it is stupid." You will likely have to change place, job or career to realize your unique potential. That will be hard to do.

Part Six: The penultimate dare is something we will all experience or have already, to be twentysomething. Children should be nourished and teenagers protected. But there are few imperatives for people in their 20s. Once you have graduated and found a job, you are expected to fend for yourself as an adult. Yet it is in our 20s that we have a chance to find our voice if we accept the dares described above. The people we admire usually dug deeper, took a different path, took risks, stumbled upon the idea, or love, of a lifetime in their 20s. Even if you missed that chance, this section will give you some ideas about how to get it back.

Part Seven: The final dare happens automatically — we get older. Once upon a time, being old was seen as being a less-capable adult. Nowadays, it is seen as an asset, a golden period in life where we can embrace new things, sharpen or blunt our personalities, and discover new horizons. Daring to get old is about more than simply ageing.

Every section will open with the story of somebody who embodies the journey described in that section. A Swedish ski jumper, an Austrian farmer, a lost British pop star and an African-American activist, to name a few. They are all remarkable people but not necessarily successful according to traditional metrics like money or prizes. Not all of them are famous. And they most certainly are not people you should emulate since copying is the very opposite of finding what makes you different. Their stories highlight the theme of the section and help us understand it in a real-world setting.

At the close of each section is a to-do list of recommendations to take the section theme further. Seven recommendations, to be precise.

Explore.

Find the hidden ingredients in yourself.

PART ONE

DARE TO
DIG DEEP

Marguerite Johnson was a quiet child. Not just quiet. Mute most of the time.

Living with her paternal grandmother in 1930s Arkansas, she found solace in books and would spend her days reading. Shakespeare, Dickens and Edgar Allan Poe, but also authors who, like Johnson, were African-American females, like Frances Harper and Jessie Fauset. It took until her early teens before she dared to start speaking. Inspired by a teacher who told her, "You do not love poetry, not until you speak it," it opened a new world for Johnson. She moved to California and, at the age of 16, became the first black streetcar conductor in San Francisco. She also became pregnant and gave birth to her first child at the age of 17. This was only the beginning of a long struggle. She married an electrician and aspiring musician of Caucasian origin, even though interracial relationships were frowned upon in 1950s America. She started taking dance classes and, for a few years, she and her husband formed a dance team but struggled to get recognition. The marriage lasted only three years. Divorce was equally frowned upon. As a single mother, she would sing and dance calypso music in a San Francisco nightclub to make ends meet. This is where she changed her name. Using her little brother's childhood nickname for her and keeping her married surname, Marguerite Johnson became Maya Angelou.

She kept looking for ways to make a solid living and toured Europe with an opera production, making it a point to practise the language of every country she visited. She gained fame on Broadway and in the movies but eventually left show business to focus on her first love, reading and writing. She moved to New York and studied under great authors like Rosa Guy and Paula Marshall. Then, in 1960, she listened to a speech by Martin Luther King Jr., which changed everything for her. She became a civil rights activist.

She remarried and moved with her husband to Ghana, where she met Malcolm X. She would help him build the Organization of Afro-American Unity when she returned to America. Disaster struck when Malcolm X was assassinated and Angelou felt devastated and lost. Something good came out of her suffering – writing returned to her life. She wrote plays and supported herself as a market researcher. But then Martin Luther King Jr., the man who inspired her to activism, was killed in 1968, and she fell into even deeper sadness and despair. Yet it inspired her to keep writing. Urged on by friends and acquaintances, she wrote her autobiography. *I Know Why the Caged Bird Sings* was published in 1969 and became an international phenomenon. It is a coming-of-age story that illustrates how strength of character and a love of literature can help overcome racism and trauma. It was a revelation, not just of a life lived, but of a soul's long journey through darkness toward light.

It also explained why Angelou had been so quiet for many years in her childhood. She was the victim of sexual abuse by her mother's boyfriend. When she confided in her brother, the sexual abuser was convicted and later murdered. She believed her words had killed him: "I thought my voice killed him; I killed that man because I told his name. And then I thought I would never speak again because my voice would kill anyone."

When Angelou passed away in 2014, after a long life of writing, activism and creativity, she was hailed as one of American literature's great voices and a remarkable Renaissance woman.

But as she pointed out in her autobiography: "There is no greater agony than bearing an untold story inside you."

YOUR SOUL IS A MINESHAFT

We all bear untold stories inside of us, some more painful than others. Confronting them is the first, difficult step in accepting our differences. The story of Maya Angelou is not just about the courage to confront secrets but about looking far, wide and deep to find what sets you apart. It is bound to be a combination of experiences and interests. A writer with a background as a calypso singer and civil rights activist will tell a different story than a writer who dropped out of business school or journeyed through the Amazon rainforest. Digging deep is to dig differently because of how different our experiences are in this world. It is a journey inward.

The idea of a soul is more rooted in philosophy than in science. Our thoughts and consciousness are centred in the organ we know as the brain. However, 'soul' is a valuable metaphor for our inner experiences and feelings, which are not always externally evident or clear to our conscious understanding. The soul is a mineshaft. Deep, dark and mysterious. Even frightening. This analogy is beautifully depicted in the animated movie *Inside Out*. Riley, the main character, goes on an adventure inside her own mind and discovers the 'Memory Dump,' a place where memories vanish as they are forgotten. A particularly poignant scene is when Riley witnesses her once-cherished childhood toy, Bing Bong, disappear into the abyss of the Memory Dump, lost forever. Although Riley returns from her inner journey with newfound insights, the memory of Bing Bong remains lost.

Staying with the mineshaft metaphor, greater value can be found at greater depth. Coal and gravel lie near the ground, whereas diamonds and other valuable gemstones lie hundreds of kilometres underneath the surface. Maya Angelou grew up as an African-American woman when racial prejudice and segregation were rampant. Yet, skin colour doesn't differentiate us; rather, it groups us into broad categories like 'ethnicity.' In the 1930s, nearly 10% of Americans, amounting to over ten million people, were African American. Many faced severe injustices, even more so than Angelou, whose grandmother remarkably built a modest fortune following the Great Depression.

Experiencing sexual assault is deeply traumatic, leaving long-lasting scars on survivors. Tragically, hundreds of thousands of individuals, predominantly women, endure similar experiences each year.

Neither skin colour nor trauma made Angelou different. It made her relatable.

The crucial component here is writing, not only because it lets others discover who you are, it also helps you explore your inner world. It can heal the things that hurt, help you remember suppressed or forgotten memories, and create a sense of cohesion. Your life was not just a random stream of chaotic events, it had a red thread, a purpose.

Yet, writing is not automatic. It takes focus and effort.

Had Angelou's calypso career been successful, *I Know Why the Caged Bird Sings* might never have seen the light of day.

Success, while desirable, can be an inhibitor — an excuse to avoid pain and confront our true selves. We win a competition, but we do not create and contribute.

There is no better example of this than the fictional millionaire Jay Gatsby.

WHAT LIES BENEATH

In *The Great Gatsby* by F. Scott Fitzgerald, Jay Gatsby's life illustrates the battle between our true selves and the personas we create for the world. He is wealthy and holds extravagant parties, but underneath lie unattainable dreams, heartbreak and secrets. Originating as James Gatz from North Dakota, he transforms himself, believing wealth and status could reclaim his lost love, Daisy Buchanan. His mansion and parties might seem like symbols of success, but they hide his deep loneliness and the gap between his cherished memories and reality. At the heart of this yearning is the green light he often stares at across the bay, a beacon symbolizing something forever just out of reach. Gatsby's pursuit of Daisy becomes less about genuine love and more about an obsession with the past. Despite his shady dealings, there's a naiveté to him. He believes that with enough effort, he can achieve his dreams. However, as Fitzgerald reminds us, sometimes our past is beyond our grasp and we are forced to "beat on, boats against the current, borne back ceaselessly into the past."

Similarly, Maya Angelou's calypso career could have landed her in some gilded Beverly Hills mansion with her story buried underneath.

The two giants of modern psychology, Sigmund Freud and his estranged protégé Carl Jung, each had a metaphor for these hidden parts of ourselves that we are blind to.

Freud likened our consciousness to an iceberg where the small tip is what we are aware of, the subconscious underneath the surface holds the desires, secret memories and suppressed experiences that shape who we are.

Jung likened our secret selves to a shadow that grew increasingly blacker and denser the more we ignored it. Jay Gatsby tries to replace his shadow with grand parties, expensive clothes and money. Instead of confronting his hidden self, he gazes at a green light in the distance.

Understanding and accepting the complexities of our inner lives is at odds with the current fixation on terms like 'diversity' and 'identity', which focus mainly on superficial traits like gender or skin colour. The term 'diverse' originally described a group or collection with a wide variety. A forest with different plants and animals is diverse. Variety is not just a 'spice of life' — it is essential. Monocultural farming or forestry, which focuses on specific crops or trees, isn't sustainable in the long run. Similarly, limiting oneself to a singular music or literary genre narrows one's worldview. As author Haruki Murakami said, "If you only read the books that everyone else is reading, you can only think what everyone else is thinking."

This is why the modern interpretation of diversity is unfortunate. Skin colour, gender and ethnicity are things no one chooses. They are chance outcomes, and while society should indeed strive to counteract any disadvantages tied to these factors, claiming that a particular ethnicity or gender automatically leads to diverse thinking is misleading. Assuming that minorities inherently possess specific qualities, regardless of intent, can perpetuate positive stereotypes as much as negative ones.

This is why we should consider 'Deep Diversity.' Rather than focusing on surface-level traits, it emphasizes our core beliefs and thoughts. Unlike our birthplace or family background, which we can't change, deep diversity is something we can cultivate over time. Peter Thiel, the cofounder of PayPal and a somewhat controversial technology investor, offers an insightful measurement of this inner differentiation. He asks job interviewees: "What important truth do very few people agree with you on?" This question stumps many, as we tend to view truths as societal constructs passed down like age-old wisdom rather than individual realizations.

However, historically, revolutionary thinkers have shattered such accepted knowledge. For instance, Copernicus questioned the widely accepted belief that the Earth was the centre of the universe, and Rachel Carson shed light on the unnoticed consequences of pesticides.

Thiel's question gauges deep diversity, free of superficial bias.

Embracing contrarian thinking and seeking out personal truths is challenging. It's not about finding one definitive answer; it's a continuous journey full of uncertainties. Think of it more as a mystery to be explored rather than a puzzle to be solved.

SOLVING PUZZLES OR UNRAVELLING MYSTERIES?

Many people have struggled with something like a 3,000-piece puzzle of, say, the Matterhorn. You work slowly and meticulously, trying out piece by piece and comparing it with the image on the box. It is a quest for coherence, where fitting together the disparate pieces unveils a predetermined image. We may sigh in frustration, but there is solace in knowing that a complete picture exists. With perseverance, every piece will find its niche, mirroring the image on the box.

A mystery stands in stark contrast. It provides no reference image, pre-established theme or a finite set of pieces. Professor Gregory Treverton articulates this distinction, saying, "[A mystery] poses a question that has no definitive answer because the answer is [unpredictable]; it hinges on the future convergence of myriad factors, both known and unknown."

Life, especially when written about in biographies, is presented as a puzzle. With the benefit of hindsight, Maya Angelou's biography looks like a chain of pivotal events, a trajectory leading to her iconic status. This portrayal simplifies life into a sequence of events, reducing its myriad complexities to a neat, linear narrative — a moralistic fable and prescriptive journey. In doing so, not only is life's richness undermined, but a sense of entitlement is fostered, making success seem an inevitable consequence.

Mysteries lack such certainties. They represent the uncharted — like a tunnel through an iceberg, echoing with shadows and uncertainties. Eric Weinstein, a mathematician, poignantly notes, "... most of us die never having heard our own voices." This unsettling reality diverges from the comforting, albeit delusional, view of life as a puzzle with guaranteed solutions. To accentuate the perils of the mysterious, myths and tales warn us of looming threats: dragons safeguarding treasures and labyrinths concealing minotaurs. Navigating this realm demands confronting our deepest fears and internal demons.

Angelou, grappling with the traumatic memories of sexual violence, believed that her silence would bury her pain and protect the world from the potency of her voice. She sought refuge in singing and dancing. She even relocated to Africa. Yet, her ultimate redemption lay in facing her torment. Think about the profound courage this act necessitated.

Most of us, indeed, exit life without truly recognizing our own voice. Not because we don't have one, but because finding it requires too much of us.

WRITING IS EXCAVATION

Words do something to us and with us. It is the only way to freeze time, putting words to the stream of random events unfolding before us. It is a way to heal or harm ourselves and others. It is a way to convey what we see and feel to others, just like telepathy. In the context of this section, it is an excavator. Our brain is full of data. Memories — some clear, some hazy — ideas, words and daydreams. When we write, we sort through these piles of data and try to identify useful things. A brilliant idea gained in a drunken stupor tends to be less useful the morning after. We may recall the blissful "Eureka!" shouted over the noise in a crowded bar when the idea hit us ("Hear me out guys, tattoo studios ... but for children!"). But when we write it down, we realize that alcohol-induced euphoria was playing tricks on us. Similarly, the moments that have haunted us lose some of their power when written down. And when we write about our tormentors, we discover things we may not have seen before. Hidden behind a memory was another memory. While our writing may be fiction, we cannot lie. The words are there on the page to convey some kind of meaning, good or bad. Right or wrong. The key element of Angelou's story is the fact that she took the time to write about her experience. Not just to write it. But to learn to write it down. By reading extensively, she honed her excavation tools — her way with words — in her work as a singer, market researcher and activist.

THE ENDLESS JOURNEY

Life has an endpoint for us all. Before that, our lives can and will move in many different directions. We will face pleasure and pain, as well as luck of both kinds. When we tell a story about a life, we reduce these complexities into a narrative arc. Maya Angelou was not a perfect person. Her writing and political beliefs have been criticized by many. Fictional characters, like Jay Gatsby, can be simplified for the purpose of storytelling. Real lives cannot. This is why digging deep is, in essence, an eternal task. There is no fixed bottom of the soul's mineshaft wherein all our mysteries and contradictions are resolved. Ultimately, this makes human beings interesting but living painful. We surprise ourselves. We change our minds. We do things despite knowing better. Our goal should not be to finish a journey but to enrich it constantly. In practical terms, this means taking time for introspection. It means journalling, meditating, engaging in honest dialogues with ourselves, and sometimes seeking external guidance to help us navigate our internal landscapes. The process can be uncomfortable, but it is through this discomfort that growth occurs. Dig deep into your own story, embrace your past, and allow the insights gained to guide your future. This is not just a journey of self-exploration — it's a pathway to leaving a unique imprint on the world, much like Maya Angelou did.

CONCLUSION: STRANGERS TO OURSELVES

To truly stand out is not just to seek what sets us apart — it is to engage deeply with the pieces of ourselves that are universally human yet uniquely ours.

Suppression is a natural part of growing up. We would be unbearable to others and ourselves if we were to live out every urge, instinct and burdensome memory daily. Exploring the parts of you that made you who you are is not about wallowing in pain or, for that matter, getting more followers by showing off your wounds and scars, as social media would have you believe.

In addition, most books about exceptional people read more like fairytales, wherein one particular event turned it all around and made the protagonist — a famous genius, maverick or both — a hero. Life as a puzzle to solve, not a mystery to explore.

In reality, the depths of us — the mineshaft — hold many clues as to who we are and what sets us apart, scattered on different depths. Exploring these depths should not be seen as a quest to excel at or succeed in. As novelist Joan Didion wrote in an essay:

> I think we are well advised to keep on nodding terms with the people we used to be, whether we find them attractive

company or not. Otherwise, they turn up unannounced and surprise us, come hammering on the mind's door at 4 a.m. of a bad night and demand to know who deserted them, who betrayed them, who is going to make amends. We forget all too soon the things we thought we could never forget. We forget the loves and the betrayals alike, forget what we whispered and what we screamed, forget who we were.

Maya Angelou's journey, from silence to acclaim, teaches us that confronting our hidden depths, though terrifying, is where our power lies. Jay Gatsby, in his relentless pursuit of an idealized past, lost himself in the superficial trappings of wealth and status. Instead of confronting his past, he built façades to hide behind. Such a life may shine brightly, but it lacks depth and true connection.

Though one of these people is fictional and the other real, they have one thing in common: they were both outsiders, a concept that the next section will study more closely.

Angelou reminds us that being an outsider isn't necessarily about feeling disconnected from society. It's about the audacity to tread where few dare, to embrace the mysteries within, and to harness them to make an indelible impact on the world.

If you want to compete, find the things that set you apart.
If you want to create, find the things that make you relatable.

Dare to dig deep.

SEVEN WAYS TO DIG DEEP

1. WRITE
   Give your inner life a voice. Write a secret journal or an online blog. Make it a regular feature of your life. Don't aspire to greatness. Rather, write something down every day no matter how bad it is. Let your inner voice surprise you.

2. ACCEPT WHO YOU USED TO BE
   It was you, even if you do not recognize that person any longer. You don't have to love them. Just be on nodding terms with them.

3. SHINE A LIGHT ON YOUR MONSTERS
   The things that hurt you may lie far back in the past. Find them and shine a spotlight on them. You will find that, over time, they can be tamed and are harmless. They may even become your friends. Or guides.

4. DO THINGS WITHOUT KNOWING WHY
   There are many reasons not to go to Ghana. Or Sweden. Ignore the reasons. Do it anyway. Some things make sense only in the long run.

5. CRAFT YOUR OWN TRUTHS BUT
   TEST THEM RELENTLESSLY

   Let your own voice see the world in new ways, but share your thoughts with others. They may agree or disagree. They may be confused, even offended. Let others challenge your truths. Don't fight too hard to keep them, just let go and find other insights. As the Haitian proverb states, "Beyond mountains there are mountains."

6. IGNORE THE SURFACE

   Our appearance – from ethnicity, dimensions and gender – is down to chance. Ignore and dig deeper to understand what people are really like.

7. SEE YOURSELF AS AN ETERNAL MYSTERY,
   NOT A FINITE PUZZLE

   Remove all end points. Dig deeper. And sideways.

Embark.

Take a trip to the outside edge.

PART TWO

DARE TO BE
AN OUTSIDER

For Mary Grandin, the teenage years were some of the most unpleasant times of her life. She was bullied in school, with fellow students yelling 'tape recorder' after her because of her repetitive way of speaking. When she fought back, throwing a book at a student who taunted her, she was expelled. Mary, or Temple, which was the middle name her parents used because there were several other Marys among the family's acquaintances, had been different from a young age. She did not speak until the age of three, had heightened sensitivity to touch, and had great difficulty with social situations. This was 1960s America and many years before autism was a widely accepted diagnosis. Grandin's only formal diagnosis in childhood had been 'brain damage,' and her parents bitterly disagreed on the best treatment for her. Her father favoured the standard medical advice at the time, institutionalization. Her mother took her to special needs doctors and speech therapists. She would also encourage Grandin's creative side, and together, they would do art projects, like carving pumpkins and making costumes for Halloween. "She had a very good sense of what I'd be able to handle and what I would not be able to handle," Grandin recalls.

When Grandin was 14, her parents divorced, and she would spend summers on a farm owned by her mother's new boyfriend. That is where her special needs became an extraordinary gift.

Having difficulty with abstractions, like algebra, Temple Grandin developed visual thinking and would see the world in photorealistic pictures, not abstract narratives. With her heightened sensitivity, she would empathize with the farm animals, as they also live in a sensory-based world. Her first-hand experiences of the anxiety of feeling threatened by everything in her surroundings and of being dismissed and feared enabled her to consider how cattle treatment could be improved to treat the livestock more humanely. With the support of her mother and the mentors she met in the higher education system, she would graduate from university with degrees in psychology and animal science. She went on a quest to change how farm animals were treated. She realized that farmers, too, were uninterested in abstractions like 'management.' They wanted things to implement, not words to remember. As she later put it: "I started on something specific. Verbal thinkers overgeneralize — big grand principles — but how do you implement these big principles?"

She started designing new facilities, like curved corrals, adapted to how cattle naturally move, reducing animal stress. She would write to industry periodicals about her designs and, slowly but surely, made farmers aware of better ways to do their work. The most significant breakthroughs took over 20 years, but by the mid-1990s, big companies like McDonald's made animal welfare part of their strategy.

Temple Grandin is today an award-winning pioneer in animal behaviour and agriculture. She has published more than 60 academic papers and still consults with the food industry about how to keep improving the treatment of farm animals.

Furthermore, she is an autism spokesperson who has helped reduce the stigma associated with the diagnosis. What was once considered a disability is now considered neurodiverse.

In her 60s, she finally underwent an MRI brain scan. No brain damage was found.

A GLASS WALL
OR A LENS?

Humans are hardwired to fit in. Our ancestors lived in groups because it improved their chances of survival. Those who were ostracized from their groups faced a higher risk of death. Conforming to group norms was thus beneficial. Our brains have evolved to reward conformity with positive feelings and punish deviations with negative ones. This is evident in brain scans. Studies have shown that when people conform to group opinions, the reward centre in the brain is activated, suggesting a neurological basis for the pleasant feelings associated with conformity.

Conversely, the anterior cingulate cortex, a part of the brain associated with detecting errors and feeling social rejection, becomes more active when people go against the group consensus. Humans are also equipped with so-called 'mirror neurons.' These brain cells fire when an individual acts, and they observe the same action performed by another. Some researchers believe mirror neurons facilitate empathy and understanding, leading to more harmonious group dynamics and a natural inclination to align oneself with others.

Some researchers take this a step further, with the sociologist Erving Goffman arguing that, "... when we are born, we are thrust onto a stage called everyday life, and our socialization consists of learning how to play our assigned roles from other people. We enact our roles in the company of others, who are, in turn, enacting their roles in interaction with us." Our entire lives, in other words, are quests to fit in and be liked, according to Goffman.

Imagine then the pain of individuals like Temple Grandin, who struggle to fit in. Consider living in a world where your entire existence seems to contradict thousands of years of evolution, with medical science offering no better verdict than 'brain damage' and recommending confinement in a mental institution. In recent years, the term 'outsider' has been glamorized and reserved for rebels and eccentric misfits — think commercials promoting laptops or sneakers. Such portrayals make being an outsider appear as a coveted badge of distinction or a branding exercise. In reality, it often signifies profound shame and isolation.

This sentiment was eloquently expressed by the character Taylor Mason in the TV show *Billions*. Taylor is a brilliant financial analyst and a mathematical genius. They — Taylor's preferred pronoun — are nonbinary and often grapple with finding their place in the world, feeling as if they are stuck behind a glass wall. This struggle is recognized and addressed by the show's protagonist, Bobby Axelrod. A candid, self-made billionaire, Axelrod grew up street-smart on the rough side of town. He discerns the strengths that Taylor's feelings of alienation bring, telling them: "What you don't realize, Taylor, is that the glass — it's not a barrier, but a lens. It's an asset. It's what makes you good. You see things differently. That's an edge." Being an outsider has its drawbacks, but it can also provide a unique perspective that others might overlook. This perspective offers significant advantages in the business world.

When the BBC produced a TV series about self-made millionaires in the United Kingdom, they undertook a comprehensive study to uncover the common traits of these entrepreneurs. Remarkably, 40% were dyslexic, and many also fell on the autism spectrum. The list of renowned business figures with such conditions is extensive. Elon Musk has publicly disclosed his diagnosis of Asperger's, which the Diagnostic and Statistical Manual of Mental Disorders or DSM for short — a US publication widely respected by the global medical community — rebranded as autism spectrum disorder in 2013. Richard Branson, the brains behind the Virgin brand, spanning everything from airlines to hotels, has often referred to his dyslexia as a 'secret superpower.' Ingvar Kamprad, the founder of IKEA, assigned his furniture unique Swedish names because his dyslexia made working with conventional inventory numbers challenging. As the BBC study highlighted, "Due to their academic struggles, many found themselves on the periphery of mainstream social groups during their school years. Feeling isolated, they compensated by exploring diverse ideas, mastering new strategies, and tirelessly seeking their own unique success blueprint." Their disadvantages became a lens, not just a wall.

CIRCLES,
NOT PYRAMIDS

The traditional view of how power is organized is a pyramid, with the ruler or CEO on top and then layers upon layers of subordinates. With an origin in Greek to describe a sacred ruler, it is not a particularly accurate description of how people experience power every day in, say, an office or schoolyard. A better way of describing that kind of power dynamics is a large circle with a smaller one inside it, like a fried egg sunny side up. The egg yolk symbolizes the insiders. The people who get invited to parties, who are admired, who get asked for their opinion and get seen. The egg white is the outsiders, those who live life uninvited. What is unnerving is that the rules to get into the inner clique — the yolk — or thrown out of it are unclear and constantly changing. Sometimes, it is connected to actual accomplishments, while at other times, it comes down to abstractions like, "That person just feels right," or "She just doesn't have the X-factor." A CEO is often, though not always, qualified through their experience. A ruler by tradition. A prime minister by an election. The journey between insider and outsider is significantly more mysterious.

People who don't fit into the current expectations of society find themselves on the outside.

Attention deficit disorder, another diagnosis in DSM, has been on the rise over the past decades not because people have significantly worsened attention spans but because modern society requires of us — especially if we are in school — to pay closer attention over longer periods of time. Who we are is out of sync with current expectations. It is an evolutionary mismatch. Another group facing ostracism and feeling like an outsider is people with obesity. In a wealthy nation, people with weight challenges tend to be viewed as less attractive and slaves to their urges. The greatest number of obese people in the US and UK are found in relatively poor areas, not rich ones. This was not always so. Once upon a time, a large body was a sign of wealth and power, whereas skinny or muscular people were viewed as weak or simple labourers. There are still so-called fattening rooms in emerging nations like Nigeria, where people go to gain a lot of weight. Similar to a gym but with a different bodily ideal being aspired to. The insiders were once outsiders and vice versa.

Some people are outsiders not because of a neurological condition or particular body shape but because they are kicked out of a group. In the case of musician Bob Geldof, he was the kind of outsider who had once been an insider, his success replaced by a sense of failure.

THE OUTSIDE EDGE

By the early 1980s, Bob Geldof's musical career was dwindling. While he had achieved chart success with his punk band, The Boomtown Rats, in the 1970s, particularly with the song "I Don't Like Mondays," by the 1980s, their releases were consistently underwhelming. The musical zeitgeist had shifted to glamorous bands like Duran Duran and Spandau Ballet. Reflecting on this period, Geldof remarked, "What a brutal business pop music is. Had the best years of my life already passed? I was worried sick. What would I do next?" With a young family, he spent more time at home than in studios or on tour. One evening, he saw a news report on the Ethiopian famine and realized the magnitude of the crisis far surpassed his personal concerns. Instead of merely writing a song and performing it himself, he sought collaboration with prominent UK pop stars. The result? "Do They Know It's Christmas?" This track raised over 20 million dollars for Ethiopia and established the genre of the charity single.

The subsequent Live Aid concert, Geldof's brainchild, grabbed global attention. The once-sidelined artist became an international icon, later knighted for his philanthropy. From being an outsider, Geldof found himself back in the heart of the establishment. This transformational journey of Geldof's closely parallels insights from another domain: science. Science historian Thomas Kuhn emphasized that fringe ideas, not mainstream ones, fuel the progress of science. These concepts originate from entities initially perceived as outliers or dissenters, challenging the dominant narrative. True understanding necessitates distancing oneself from the prevalent norm. Whether in science, pop music or leadership, groundbreaking ideas often germinate on the periphery.

A widely recognized example of the power of fringe ideas is the viral YouTube video "Guy Starts Dance Party" from the 2009 Sasquatch Music Festival. In the video, an initially overlooked individual's unconventional dance gradually becomes the centrepiece, drawing a massive crowd. The weird dancer becomes the mainstream. Similarly, Charles Bukowski, renowned for his stark portrayals of urban tribulations, aptly noted, "The crowd is the gathering place of the weakest; true creation is a solitary act."

This is why artists talk of the 'anxiety of influence,' the struggle emerging creators face when trying to find their unique voice amidst the overwhelming presence of their predecessors. It's easy to become enmeshed in established norms. But as the masterful painter William Blake put it: "I must create a system or be enslaved by another man's. I will not reason and compare. My business is to create." This anxiety of influence is not just an artistic concern but can be observed in settings like office meetings. Attendees come in with their own ideas and agendas, but often find themselves effortlessly swayed by the dominant voice, forgoing their unique insights.

Interestingly, the term 'idiot' originally didn't denote someone lacking judgment or intellect. Its origin, the Greek *idiōtēs*, described an individual not involved in public affairs — an outsider, someone who kept to their own. In the context of our exploration, it's poetic: the very word used today to dismiss someone's perspective historically referred to those outside the establishment. In recognizing the potency of fringe ideas, perhaps it's the modern 'idiots', the dissenters and outliers, to whom we should pay close attention. They might just be the bearers of the next groundbreaking idea.

CONCLUSION: THE BEST OR THE ONLY?

Many of us are torn between the desire to stand out and the comfort of fitting in. Adam Grant, a leading voice in organizational psychology, playfully suggests that a middle ground might be to belong to a standout group — like radical environmentalists or an extreme political faction. But behind the humour lies a deeper truth: Bridges, not barriers, between mainstream and unconventional ideas should be built. Such openness ensures that groundbreaking thoughts seep into the larger conversation. For a society to truly advance, it must champion its outliers.

The 'isolation effect' in psychology suggests that distinct items — or people — are more memorable. Picture a list dominated by fruits but with one car name thrown in; that car is what you'd likely remember. This resembles an outsider's experience: standing out, sometimes feeling isolated. Temple Grandin's journey depicts this dynamic's highs and lows.

Embracing your unique identity is a double-edged sword. It can illuminate paths less travelled and inspire others. Yet, it can also cast shadows of loneliness or draw criticism. Our next section will explore the pain that can follow when you deviate from the norm.

Do you aim to shine within established frameworks and norms?
Or seek to sketch your own canvas, unhindered by existing outlines?

Do you vie to climb the ladder everyone sees, reaching its pinnacle?
Or do you yearn to craft a space only you inhabit, unparalleled and unmatched?

Do you want to compete and be the best?
Or do you want to create and be the only one?

Dare to be an outsider.

SEVEN WAYS
TO BE AN OUTSIDER

1. CELEBRATE YOUR CHALLENGES
   The things that hold you back enable you to find other paths and see things that others miss.

2. POLISH THE LENS
   It will not be evident from the outset exactly how you see things differently. Continually share your observations with others and be prepared for pushbacks. Remember that they don't have access to the lens and will not always understand what you are on about.

3. ACKNOWLEDGE THAT MORE OPPORTUNITIES CAN BE FOUND ON THE OUTSIDE LOOKING IN
   Yes, getting invited to parties is nice. Life on the outside can be cold and lonely. Yet it is out in the wilderness that new, wild ideas reside.

4. BE AN IDIOT
   Insults are there to protect the status quo. Take pride in being called an idiot; it is a sign that you are on to something interesting, if not always correct.

5. RE-DEFINE THE BOUNDARIES TO KEEP AN OUTSIDER'S PERSPECTIVE

If you do the first four steps right, people will see your value and invite you into the inner circle. Resist. Draw a larger outside circle and stay there; it is the basis for your unique perspective. Remember that the conditions for being an insider are fickle, so take control of your life instead of being subject to the opinions of others.

6. GO TO THE FRINGES TO FIND THE NEW

Always seek out strange new offerings in art, philosophy, politics and science. If what you find makes you go "Whoa!," "Wow!" or "WTF?," it is a sign that you have found the fringe. The findings will not always be truthful, but they will push you in new directions.

7. BE THE BRIDGE

Outsiders and insiders are at odds with each other. You can be the link between them. Express yourself politely. Listen more than you speak. Don't label others or yourself. Take the rest of us on a journey. Share what you see, think and believe. Bridge gaps.

Embrace.

Use tough times to shape you.

PART THREE

DARE TO SUFFER

Jan Boklöv was born in the cold and made his name in the cold. Hailing from Lapland in northernmost Sweden, he lived next to a ski jump slope, the main hangout after school for Boklöv and his friends. Once he had let go of his fears of the high tower, its steep gradient, and the idea of flying dozens of metres on a pair of skis, he went daily. He even got into a high school specializing in the sport. He started competing and was an average practitioner, often managing around 75 metres when the best made over 90-metre-long jumps. One day, in 1985, everything changed. His skis, held together parallel as the sport stipulated with marks for both length and aesthetic beauty of the jump, drifted apart mid-air by the air pressure and formed a V. He registered his first 90-metre jump. He tried it again. Even farther. A new style of ski jumping had been born. The V-style. It took him more than a year of experimentation to perfect it. Even though spectators laughed at him and judges consistently gave him low marks for aesthetics, he persevered. He looks like a flappy bird, one commentator remarked.

Nevertheless, Boklöv went from an also-ran to winning the Ski Jump World Cup in 1988–1989. It changed the sport entirely, and by the 1992 Winter Olympics, all participants had adopted the style, making Boklöv's advantage redundant. He finished in 47th place.

Boklöv's flights were not just a test of athletic ingenuity; they were battles against an invisible foe that haunted him from within, epilepsy. One chilling day, as Boklöv ascended into the skies, a seizure took hold, turning a triumphant leap into a harrowing plummet.

It would be tempting to weave a narrative that epilepsy was the crucible from which Boklöv's genius emerged, as history is replete with luminaries who bore its mark — from Julius Caesar and Fyodor Dostoevsky to the abolitionist Harriet Tubman and rapper Lil Wayne to name a few. But that would be a romantic oversimplification. For epilepsy isn't a divine spark or a gifted touch; it's a beast of unpredictability, a shadowy affliction that can strike without warning, turning ordinary moments into dangerous battlegrounds. It serves in this section as an example of how being different, an outlier, often goes together with pain and suffering.

TRAPEZE ARTISTS

Elite sportspeople, like Jan Boklöv, are more likely to experience mental health disorders. A large study of Canadian national athletes found that over 40% met the criteria for depression, anxiety and/or an eating disorder. When we admire the talents displayed in sports, we often fail to grasp just how large the sacrifices are and the dangers involved. This is not the only spectacle with hidden stakes. To understand the hazards in something as seemingly mundane as stand-up comedy, consider the metaphors used when something goes awry. If a joke doesn't land well or, God forbid, you offend the entire audience, terms like 'crash and burn' and 'to bomb' come into play. A notorious instance occurred when Michael Richards, who portrayed Kramer on the TV show *Seinfeld*, performed a stand-up routine in Los Angeles. He grew irritated with some audience members and retaliated by heckling them, taking greater liberties — and greater risks —with his words. His frustration escalated to the point where he hurled racist insults. The laughter in the room turned to gasps of shock. Richards' career as a stand-up comedian never recovered from this incident; he had truly crashed and burned.

Stand-up comedians are akin to trapeze artists, perpetually taking risks, teetering on the edge of social acceptability. Veer too far, and they plummet; restrain too much, and they become mundane and predictable. In either scenario, the result is a humourless failure.

Artistry, in its essence, is also a balancing act. Figures like Vincent van Gogh, Frida Kahlo and Beethoven serve as poignant examples — artists who channelled their inner pain and physical ailments to elevate their work.

Lol Tolhurst, a founding member of the gloomy rock band The Cure, puts it eloquently:

> There comes a day when every single one of us is confronted with the abyss. Sometimes it's a heart-wrenching breakup. Sometimes it's the loss of a loved one. Some have it early and some people get it late, but we all have that moment when we look down and there's nothing fucking there. People want their rock stars to go further out on the edge and hang out there for a bit, take a good long look at that abyss, and then transmit what they find there through their art.

This is precisely why we hold the work of painters, singers, athletes and stand-up comedians in such high regard. They venture where many won't, placing themselves on a precarious ledge like a trapeze artist suspended high above the circus floor. The pivotal word to grasp here is 'balance.' Lean too much in either direction, and the unique perspective that sets an artist apart fades away. Worse, the effects become corrosive to the individual — a curse, not a blessing.

SUSTAINABLY DIFFERENT

Friedrich Nietzsche wrote in *Thus Spoke Zarathustra* that, "… one must have chaos in oneself to give birth to a dancing star." This is a common misunderstanding in artistic endeavours — that you must be what you create. There's an anecdote from the filming of *Marathon Man* in the 1970s where Dustin Hoffman, famed for his method acting, deprived himself of sleep to emulate his character's exhaustion. Upon seeing Hoffman's ragged state, the seasoned Sir Laurence Olivier supposedly quipped, "Have you tried acting, dear boy? It's much easier." Though the authenticity of this exchange remains contested, the underlying lesson has resonated deeply in acting circles: "Emulate madness, don't embody it."

The perils of such immersion aren't exclusive to actors. Trent Reznor, the luminary behind Nine Inch Nails, crafted a persona for his album *The Downward Spiral*. Through it, he channelled the anguish of a fractured psyche desperate for solace. Released amid the early 1990s recession and the poignant tones of the grunge movement, the album's themes of self-destruction and despair resonated deeply. But the line between Reznor and his creation blurred, leading him down a path marred by addiction. He survived, but others, like the frontmen of Nirvana and Soundgarden, weren't as fortunate. Playing with the fire of such raw emotions can sear the soul if not handled judiciously.

Emotion should inspire the art, not consume it; it should be the well, not the water.

Similarly, while U2 was working on the album *Achtung Baby*, guitarist Dave 'The Edge' Evans channelled the heartbreak of his crumbling marriage into the track "Love Is Blindness." Driven by raw pain, he unleashed a visceral guitar solo, but the end result fell flat. In its final form, the solo was transformed into a restrained, somber tune — a stark portrayal of love's void. Once again, this underscores the notion that pain should be the muse, not the medium.

But pain is not as dramatic and prone to romanticizing as this.

Pain should not be glorified, it should be endured.

SHADES OF SUFFERING

If there was an absolute scale of human discomfort and only the gravest pain was allowed to be called 'suffering,' few would suffer. Like all emotions, pain and suffering are subjective. Most of us lead regular lives, far from the glamour of the sports arena or concert stage. We face everyday challenges. Sometimes we are frustrated over the lack of 5G coverage or the number of days left before a pay day. Sometimes we just feel down. Most of the time, everyday pain comes from loneliness and boredom.

A French scientist from the 1600s, Blaise Pascal, said that people's problems come from being unable to sit alone quietly. This idea is even more true today. We're always checking our phones, afraid we're missing out on something. In fact, a large study of smartphone use found that one of the main reasons for frequent checking of email, likes or news headlines was to avoid feeling bored. Yet, the word 'boredom' didn't even exist in Pascal's time. It came around in the 1850s when big changes like factories and city living took place. These changes gave people more free time, and sometimes, that led to boredom. But being bored isn't always bad. Think about famous people like Isaac Newton and J.K. Rowling. They came up with their great ideas when they had time to think. Boredom can be like a blank canvas, inviting us to think deeply and be creative. This also requires a balancing act. Spending too much time alone can be risky. Your thoughts can go in circles and make you feel trapped. Being too much in your own head can twist how you see the world. This can be dangerous, as some people have done terrible things because they got lost in their thoughts, believing that their way of seeing the world was the only right way to see the world.

The key is to find a balance. Use moments of boredom to inspire you, but be careful not to get lost in your own thoughts. It's a challenging balance, but it's possible for the trapeze artist in all of us, unless we are Homer Simpson.

LONELY ARE
THE ONLY

In a famous episode of *The Simpsons*, Homer discovers that the source of his stupidity is that he has a crayon lodged in his brain. He had inserted it through his nose as a child and forgotten about it. He has it surgically removed and instantly becomes a genius. The only person he can bond with is his equally gifted daughter Lisa. He becomes terribly lonely and has difficulty keeping up with the idiocy of the people around him. His gift enables him to see shortcomings in his workplace, a nuclear power plant, and the report he writes to authorities forces the plant to shut down, leaving Homer's former colleagues jobless. Lost and alone, Homer realizes that due to his improved intelligence, he is no longer welcome, and his life was more enjoyable when he was an idiot. In the end, he has the crayon put back into his brain. The first words uttered when he wakes from anesthesia, and proof that the surgery has been a success, are: "Extended warranty, how can I lose?!"

Being gifted is isolating and its fruits — money, fame, accolades — even more so. Dreaming of success fails to imagine the effects of success. They can be remarkably difficult. Tennessee Williams beautifully captures this sentiment in the poignantly named essay "The Catastrophe of Success." In it, he explores the loneliness and emptiness that often trail behind the glittering facade of success. Williams argues that success can be disorienting, distancing one from the very essence of life that once provided solace and meaning:

> The sort of life that I had had previous to this popular success was one that required endurance, a life of clawing and scratching along a sheer surface and holding on tight with raw fingers to every inch of rock higher than the one caught hold of before, but it was a good life because it was the sort of life for which the human organism is created. I was not aware of how much vital energy had gone into this struggle until the struggle was removed. I was out on a level plateau with my arms still thrashing and my lungs still grabbing at air that no longer resisted. [...] I sat down and looked about me and was suddenly very depressed.

When the things you battled for a long time are removed, the void created can make you yearn for more suffering. Or as Vietnamese author Thích Nhất Hạnh puts it: "People have a hard time letting go of their suffering. Out of fear of the unknown, they prefer suffering that is familiar."

When people achieve success or, in Homer Simpson's case, the intelligence they've lacked, they may cling to old pains and familiar sufferings simply because it's what they know.

This paradox, where success or newfound intelligence can lead to unexpected emptiness or suffering, reminds us that sometimes, what we yearn for the most might not bring the happiness or sense of belonging we anticipate. The search, too, is a balancing act.

CONCLUSION: THE PEACOCK

Imagine if Bob Dylan, the Nobel prize-winning musician and icon, was unknown and performed in a talent show, like *American Idol* or *Britain's Got Talent*. He would most likely fail miserably. You can imagine judges and audience members alike looking confused as the moody singer monotonously and atonally delivered his strange lyrics. Most likely, he would not even make it to the next round. A competition rewards those who fit in. Comparison is not only a thief of joy but originality.

The evolutionary theory known as the 'Survival of the Fittest' has a sneaky little secret: the word 'fit.' We usually associate it with fitness, especially in the context of a species' survival. The strong and fit live to see another day or millennium. But the word also denotes fitting in, adapting to one's surroundings, and being one among many. This is why the peacock is such a strange bird. In theory, according to the Survival of the Fittest, it should not exist.

It can't fly and must carry around an enormous tail. The greater the tail, the greater its success in mating. The theory of the evolutionary success of the peacock is that it leads a difficult life, and the difficulty impresses others. It is sexy, not fit. It does not fit in, it stands out.

Pain, like the peacock's tail, is a heavy burden. We seek ways to avoid it — both in its dramatic manifestations and when it comes from the mere dullness of existence. Yet, it brings beauty. And inspiration. It is truly a double-edged sword. Or perhaps that saying should be changed to "it is truly a peacock's tail."

Jan Boklöv's jumping style was deemed unaesthetic by the head of the Global Ski Association, FIS.

Frida Kahlo's art was overshadowed by her husband, Diego Rivera, in her lifetime. He is long forgotten and she is viewed as a legend.

Vincent Van Gogh struggled with mental health issues and poverty. He only sold a few paintings while alive and was not widely recognized in the art world. His unique style, celebrated today, was avant-garde for his time and did not meet the tastes of art critics or the general public.

In a world where conformity often seems like the path of least resistance, Boklöv, Kahlo and Van Gogh are the peacocks that remind us of the beauty, pain and profound potential of daring to be different.

Do you want to compete and fit neatly into the status quo?
Or do you want to be a peacock?

Dare to be in pain.

SEVEN WAYS TO SUFFER

1. ACCEPT PAIN

   We are programmed as human beings to avoid pain. We should not glorify it, but we need to accept it. The price of being an outsider is pain — dramatic or mundane. Accept it without judging it.

2. BUT DON'T ROMANTICIZE IT

   Yes, famous people have suffered. That does not mean suffering is a prerequisite to creation —quite the opposite. Sometimes, they persevered despite the pain, not because of it.

3. BE BORED!

   Boredom is the kind of everyday pain we can all endure. Stay in it, don't escape. Take a break from stimuli. Stay off the smartphone for an hour every now and then. Let weekends and holidays be celebrations of boredom, not always a constant rush to new adventures and experiences.

4. DISTINGUISH BETWEEN LONELINESS AND SOLITUDE

Loneliness is distressing. We are social creatures. But solitude — being alone with your thoughts — is a healthy, necessary way to cope with a hyperconnected, always-on world. Make time for solitude. Remember, you are not alone.

5. CREATE YOUR OWN PEACOCK'S TAIL

Find a symbol of the thing that sets you apart. It could be a clothing item, a way of speaking, a ritual, or another way of being different. If it provokes some people, it is bound to attract others.

6. DON'T DREAM OF A DAY WHEN IT'S ALL OVER

You may accomplish great things but your feelings of being different and the pain will never fully subside. Too much success may aggravate them. Fantasize less, endure more.

7. WALK *WITH* YOUR DEMONS

Pain is an energy. Run away from it and you risk running astray. Lean too much into it and the pain consumes you. Walk with it. See it as a fire to be managed. It takes constant movement to be completely balanced, like a trapeze artist.

Enlighten.

Look further, be greater.

PART FOUR

DARE TO
BE KIND

Franz Jägerstätter lived close to heaven, high in the Austrian Alps, where faith ran deep. But he was not a religious man at first. His youth was marked by rebellion and exuberance. Intelligent and adventurous, he was the village's first to own a motorcycle, gaining a reputation as a spirited young man with a penchant for fun and fights. He would have lived an unremarkable, ordinary life had it not been for two transformative shifts. In the mid-1930s, his life took a sharp turn toward spirituality, so suddenly that many believed him to be "possessed by a higher power." Marriage to the deeply pious Franziska only deepened his faith, and a pilgrimage to Rome to receive the Pope's blessings solidified his commitment.

The year 1938 brought darkness to Austria. As German troops marched in and the country voted for the Anschluss, Jägerstätter stood alone in his village, the sole voice of dissent. He rejected Nazi ideologies, a stance that made him an outlier even among his fellow Catholics. The world around him seemed to have lost its moral compass, but he remained unwavering.

Conscripted in 1943 and faced with the atrocities of the Nazi regime, Jägerstätter's conscience wouldn't allow him to fight. Despite pleas from friends and the haunting reality of leaving behind his wife and three young daughters, he refused to swear loyalty to Hitler. His quiet act of defiance landed him in prison, where he faced execution. But even in his final moments, when offered a chance to save his life, he chose integrity over compromise, sealing his fate with a love for God and humanity that few could fathom.

Franz Jägerstätter was kind. But his kindness is one of conviction and courage. Long misunderstood and criticized, his story remained in the shadows until it found recognition in books, films, and finally, beatification[2] by the Catholic Church in 2007.

When the filmmaker Terrence Malick portrayed Jägerstätter's life, he called the film *A Hidden Life*, based on the following quote by author George Eliot, or Mary Anne Evans, which was her real name: "The growing good of the world is partly dependent on unhistoric acts; and that things are not so ill with you and me as they might have been, is half owing to the number who lived faithfully a hidden life, and rest in unvisited tombs."

This section is about daring to find kindness in a world that often rewards the opposite.

2   Beatification in the Catholic Church is the declaration that a person is 'Blessed,' a step toward sainthood.

RUTHLESSNESS, MEDIA AND THE SCARCITY OF KINDNESS

A time traveller from the past spending a day in today's world would assume that the modern way to get ahead is sheer ruthlessness. Business is framed as a competitive race of winners and losers. The most-admired CEOs and founders — the Musks and Jobs of the world — are frequently portrayed as all-powerful geniuses who sacrificed family and friends in pursuit of their ambitions.

Zooming out from business, media stories are full of celebrity drama and scandals, often laced with schadenfreude, as if these people had it coming.

The online world — or at least the comments section — is rife with bullying and trolling.

Influencers flaunt their status built on exclusivity and elitism.

Bidding wars determine who gets to own what and live where.

Politics has become a game of personalities with counterestablishment opinions mistaken for truth.

Cityscapes juxtapose beggars next to high-rise skyscrapers and other manifestations of inequality.

And on it goes.

The disillusioned time traveller would most certainly get back in their Delorean and return to some simpler, less connected time.

This bleak portrait is a simplification, and there may not have been a historical period to idolize, but it reminds us what a rare trait kindness is today, at least in the media-fuelled public sphere.

The governing systems we have crafted — in business and politics, at least — are governed by a narrow toolbox in the art of being human. Generosity, selflessness, kindness and forgiveness — virtues historically — have unclear benefits in these arenas. They become abstractions at best.

But, as American poet Mary Karr reminds us: "Sure, the world breeds monsters, but kindness grows just as wild."

THE KINDNESS
LANDSCAPE

In fairy tales, kindness often appears simplified: a poor woodcutter spares the life of a trapped animal and is granted three wishes in return; a prince forgives a wicked witch's misdeeds, showing kindness to someone who wronged him. These narratives and bumper sticker maxims like 'Kindness is contagious' reduce kindness to a singular act, a transaction wherein you do something for others and receive something in return.

In reality, kindness is far more complex. It is an intertwined set of behaviours, dispositions, motivations and principles that shape our interactions with ourselves, others and the world. Kindness is not a singular act but a landscape.

Consider Franz Jägerstätter's life. Many of his actions could have been perceived as selfish by those around him. Why didn't he fight in the war like others? Only later was the greater good of his actions revealed. True kindness must be difficult, and a degree of invisibility may be integral to its authenticity. The opposite of kindness isn't cruelty but insincerity.

Is it kind to lie or tell the truth?

Is it kind to collaborate or be the sole voice of dissent?

Is it kind to conform or stand out?

Is it kind to move or to stand your ground?

Viewing kindness as a landscape to explore rather than a simplistic story element or transactional tool reveals that the answers to these questions are often nuanced. It all depends on context, motivation and the intricate interplay of human emotions and ethics.

THE MOST
RADICAL ACT

Let us apply complex kindness to one of the most difficult and countercultural things you can do today: change your mind.

Understanding this challenge requires examining human biology and psychology. In a study conducted by American neuroscientists in the mid-2010s, participants with strong opinions on various subjects were examined. The participants were placed inside MRI machines, and then researchers presented counterarguments to their strongly held beliefs. Some refutations were neutral, like correcting the misconception that Thomas Edison invented the lightbulb by providing historical context. Other refutations were more politically charged, such as presenting a statement that countered a participant's belief in strict gun control.

The MRI study revealed a startling response: when confronted with counterarguments on politically charged topics, the participants' brains reacted as if facing a physical threat. This reaction triggered adrenaline release, causing physical responses similar to encountering a wild bear in the forest. The brain, in its role as protector of both the physical and psychological self, treated these challenged beliefs as if they were physical parts of the body under threat.

This physiological reaction underscores the immense challenge of re-evaluating our beliefs, particularly in today's politically polarized climate. We often perceive ourselves in a battle of good versus evil, where abandoning an entrenched position feels like an attack not just on ourselves but on our tribe.

As discussed in the section 'Dare to Be an Outsider,' humans have evolved by forming and maintaining groups, with much of our brain programming oriented toward discrimination against 'them' and favouring 'us.' Ideas and opinions thus become part of our group identity and weapons in tribal battles.

Changing your mind is a profoundly radical act precisely because it defies our biological and sociological essence as human beings.

Yet, the need to change your mind is greater than it has been in a long time, given the number of existential threats, real or perceived.

Climate change, and the intricate complexities of climate science, forces all of us to abandon entrenched positions — whether they are on the 'the world is dying' side or the 'climate change is a hoax' side — in order to find practically applicable solutions.

Digging in, clinging to dogma, calling the other side stupid because they don't understand your way of thinking in that kind of climate increases ROI — risk of ignorance.

The reason we admire certain leaders — in all fields — is because of their ability to change their minds.

Mikhail Gorbachev opened the Soviet Union to 'glasnost' (openness) and 'perestroika' (restructuring) when the old communist ways were not working.

Nelson Mandela crafted a rainbow nation of tolerance and unity, not violent revenge on the apartheid system.

Václav Havel, the Czech playwright turned president, changed his mind about political engagement, evolving from a dissident writer to a national leader guiding Czechoslovakia through a nonviolent transition from communism to democracy.

Alva Myrdal, a Swedish sociologist, diplomat and politician, shifted her focus from social welfare to disarmament. Her change in priority and subsequent work on nuclear disarmament won her the Nobel Peace Prize in 1982.

Wangari Maathai, the Kenyan environmental and political activist, founded the Green Belt Movement and shifted her focus over time to address the intricate connections between environmental sustainability, women's rights and democracy. Her evolving perspective made her an influential global voice for deep change.

And many, many others.

Whether adapting to new scientific insights, shifting policies to address emerging societal needs, or personal growth through embracing diverse viewpoints, changing one's mind is an essential tool for building a different, maybe better, future.

"

What people see as fearlessness is really persistance.

"

Wangari Maathai, *Unbowed*

LIVING ASYMMETRICALLY

The world-famous author and life coach Tony Robbins often tells the story of his childhood. His early years were fraught with struggle and adversity. His mother, gripped by addictions to drugs and alcohol, often took out her frustrations on him and his siblings, subjecting them to horrifying abuse. One haunting memory from his childhood was when his mother forced the young boy to swallow a bottle of liquid soap for swearing.

As the eldest of three siblings, Robbins took it upon himself to shield his younger family members from the cruelty of their unstable home life. The situation was further complicated by his mother's multiple remarriages, leaving the children feeling abandoned and forced to fend for themselves.

Eventually, a terrifying incident prompted him to leave home: a confrontation with his mother that escalated to the point where she chased him with a knife. This event marked both an end and a beginning, catalyzing Robbins's decision to break free from the cycle of abuse. While he never returned home, his commitment to his siblings remained unwavering.

Even more startling is that Tony Robbins always speaks about his mother with gratitude and even love. He says that whatever she did to him contributed to making him who he became.

If justice is symmetry — think of the scales in the hand of Lady Justice — then gratitude in the face of abuse is asymmetrical. There are countless stories of people who have been abused and bullied — all heartbreaking — and how they seek payback later in life.

As radical and difficult as changing your mind is the ability to live asymmetrically. Not succumbing to vengeful dreams about payback or an 'eye for an eye' mindset.

This lesson is especially apt at a time when political leaders — authoritarians in particular — paint vivid pictures of some future promised land where all our ills have been solved and every injustice dealt with. These utopias — seductive as they are — have historically led to some of the worst atrocities. The Red Khmers in Cambodia, Stalin's reign in the Soviet Union, and Nazi Germany are just a few examples.

Democracy works slowly, not with revolutionary speed. It promises no utopian vision. There is no end of history nor a final solution. As the old joke goes, the great conspiracy is that liberals are plotting to take over the world ... and leave you alone.

CONCLUSION: THE GREATER, LONGER GOOD

One of the unique human traits is the ability for abstract, long-term thinking. All animals can respond to immediate threats and some can even hoard food for the coming winter or make peace with another flock of monkeys for the purpose of survival.

But the ability to imagine things hidden years, even decades, away is — to the best of our understanding — a uniquely human ability.

This is the very foundation of what we call progress. It has enabled us to invent new modes of transporation, new ways of building houses, and new ways of collaborating across borders and cultures. Franz Jägerstätter's fate is an example of long-term thinking. And the pivots by Gorbachev, Mandela, Havel, Myrdal and Maathai. Leadership is the art of taking yourself — and others — to a place they did not know existed.

An unfortunate side effect of our modern capitalistic system, historically, is that it has rewarded the visible — sales made here and now — and disregarded future abstractions; what economists call externalities, like emissions — short-term profits in the front seat and long-term sustainability in the back. The system has been more monkey than human.

This is slowly changing in the 21st century. We are starting to ask questions about what unborn children will think of our decisions and priorities. We are opening our eyes to possibilities and threats beyond our lifetime. The system is becoming human.

In this age, complex kindness — showing an ability to change your mind, think long-term and accept imperfections — will be an asset, something that defines and differentiates you.

Do you want to compete and be just like the ruthless leaders of yesterday?

Or do you want to be a part of creating the next world?

In a world where you can be almost anything, dare to be kind!

SEVEN WAYS
TO BE KIND

1. MAKE KINDNESS COMPLEX
   Being polite and reciprocal in an interaction is simply
   a transaction. It should be a given. Kindness is richer
   and more complex than that.

2. DEFY THE NOW!
   The status quo does not like to lose its status. What
   you believe in and what sets you apart will meet op-
   position. Sometimes fierce. Take a long-term view of
   the world. It is easier than it sounds. Just add a zero
   before the year anytime you write, and voilá, you have
   a 10,000-year perspective.

3. REMEMBER THAT VALUE LIES PRIMARILY
   IN WHAT'S INVISIBLE
   Sensationalist drama and market capitalization gets
   headlines because it is direct. Real value lies hidden.
   Kind actions are not immediately rewarded.

4. MAKE A HABIT OF CHANGING YOUR MIND
   Knowledge is dead information. The things you claim
   to know may already be outdated by years, even decades. With new ways of measuring and crunching
   data emerging at an ever-faster pace, you will need to
   challenge your convictions more often.

5. DON'T BE VENGEFUL
   We all go through life with people that hurt us. When
   the pain subsides, find a way to understand the bigger
   picture. Find a way to understand why these people did
   what they did. Find a way to forgive, if not forget. Finding these ways is harder than merely extracting revenge.
   That is why they are more rewarding in the long term.

6. ACKNOWLEDGE THE MYSTERY WITHIN
   EVERYONE, INCLUDING YOURSELF
   Our inner complexities often get lost in translation, perceived by others as noise or oddity. Practice patience
   in revealing your true self, and embrace the enigma
   that resides in us all.

7. CONSIDER YOUR FUTURE SELF
   While living in the now is good for your mind, don't
   forget our human gift of foresight. Use it in your choices. Ask, "What would the me in a decade — or three
   — thank me for?"

Elevate.

Find a new vantage point
to see a new horizon.

PART FIVE

DARE TO
MOVE

Justine Frischmann wanted to become a nobody. The daughter of a Holocaust survivor, she spent her 20s as a musician and became one of the most (in)famous pop stars in the United Kingdom's 1990s music scene, known as Britpop. She founded the bands Suede and Elastica, which sold millions of albums and toured the world. Her love life turned into tabloid magazine fodder, and the intense rock 'n' roll lifestyle came with debilitating drug habits. "It always felt like a rollercoaster ride, and there was going to be a horrible smash," she recalls of those turbulent, troublesome years. Studies have shown that the average life expectancy of European pop stars is under 40 years old, so the glamorous lifestyle comes with a steep price.

When the decade ended, she'd had enough. She escaped to Boulder, Colorado, and enrolled in a master's program in visual art, expressly desiring more privacy and anonymity — to become a nobody, in her own words. Having been raised in London and seen little more than the cityscape, she had been drawn to the vast American landscapes she glimpsed through the tour bus window. At art school, she learned how to remove her ego from the creative process, the opposite of pop stardom. She started life anew, met a meteorologist and, once she graduated, moved to San Francisco. She escaped the celebrity shackles and hid from the world, but her art did not. Slowly but surely, she built a reputation as an abstract painter, winning prizes and, by 2016, was hailed as one of the top 1,000 artists alive today.

This section is about the courage and possibilities of moving — whether away from or toward something or simply shifting things around to gain a different perspective.

THE VILLAGE AND THE CITY

We didn't use to move much as human beings. Or rather, once we transitioned from being nomadic hunter-gatherers to farmers around 12,000 years ago, we often spent our entire lives in the same village where we were born. We lived and worked in the exact same way as our ancestors. Then, sometime in the mid-1800s, we began migrating to cities. What had been destiny suddenly became a decision. Stay or go? What should you work with? Whom should you marry? The past few decades have broadened these choices even further, with opportunities to live wherever you want, work from home, and marry whomever you choose — or not at all. Moving — whether to or from something or someone — has become an issue we frequently confront.

The difference between a village and a city is deeper than the mere agglomeration of buildings and number of inhabitants. Especially if we add time into the equation to understand and compare the ancient village to a modern city. The village typically had about 200 inhabitants and was governed by the seasons. The city has over a million people, ranging from the unemployed to billionaire hedge fund traders and part-time DJs. The mindset governing the village was one of cyclicality and tradition — the seasons would change predictably and control the planting of crops, the harvest and the resting period. If anyone challenged the status quo in a village, it threatened the whole community because every pair of hands was needed in the field or barn. The modern city, on the other hand, thrives on change and differentiation. If one million urban inhabitants decided tomorrow to become farmers, the entire town would collapse, and there wouldn't be enough land around for anything beyond small-scale subsistence farming. If everyone worked for the same company or industry, the city would crumble, as was the case when Detroit declined in the 2010s following the fall of the automotive industry. A city thrives because some people are baristas, others drive cabs, and another group works in banks. Movement is the oxygen that keeps the diverse city alive – changing jobs or apartments, moving to a different city or industry.

A side effect of differentiation is that cities have become havens of tolerance, with mosques standing next to synagogues, Lebanese restaurants next to sushi bars, and annual Pride parades. This has an economic impact, as urban studies theorist Richard Florida found when he correlated tolerance with innovation and prosperity. Cities with higher tolerance levels – those more open to immigrants, different ethnicities and LGBTQ+ communities – attract a more diverse talent pool. This diversity, in turn, fosters creativity, innovation and economic growth. What threatened the ancient village has become essential for the modern city. If you are going to move, it is wise to go to a place where you are tolerated, even celebrated.

This perspective can help us understand the contested Brexit referendum. The UK, and London in particular, was the only part of Europe where the four EU freedoms of movement – people, capital, goods and services – worked. From the mid-1990s until the 2010s, everyone wanted to go to London – plumbers, dancers, waiters, bankers and writers. London became a financial hub and a home to Lithuanians, Swedes and Portuguese alike. Its offerings — in food, style and music — were as rich as those in Singapore and New York. Few people dreamt of trying their luck in Bratislava or Borås. Nobody dreamt of studying in Łódź or Maribor unless they were Polish or Slovenian. Everyone had a single destination. Some people in the UK had enough of migration and the perceived loss of national identity, and blamed economic woes and crime on the UK's ability to attract people and money. It was enough to make the country vote to leave the EU in 2016. However, if only London residents had voted, the country would have remained in the EU.

It is important to remember that statistics belie individuals. Behind every figure is an individual trying to go about her life. What makes somebody move? Or stay? The answer tends to be connected to the individual's experience of their close environment, not macroeconomics.

EXPRESSIVE QUITTING

Tangping has been a Chinese trend in recent years. It translates to 'lying flat' and is used to describe a social phenomenon or lifestyle choice where individuals choose to reject the intense pressures of work and societal expectations, reverting to an idle, horizontal life as a means of protest. The Chinese are not alone in this. The majority of the world's workforce is disengaged. More specifically, 77% claim to be either quiet quitting, where an employee disengages from their work, reducing their effort and commitment, without formally resigning or communicating their dissatisfaction, or loud quitting, where they complain and formally resign. We have all been there — bad bosses, bureaucratic labyrinths, low pay, poor work-life balance, uninteresting tasks and so on. The reasons to hate your job are many.

Daring to move has the potential to lift spirits and productivity alike. Larry Gagosian's career as an art gallerist was triggered by quitting his job at a large Hollywood talent agency, comparing the airless corporate environment to a "knife fight in a phone booth." He is not the only one who flourished by quitting. Julia Childs left a career in advertising before she became a chef. Andrea Bocelli was a lawyer before he became an opera singer. Harrison Ford was a carpenter before he became an actor. Jeff Bezos worked as an investment banker in New York before quitting and, famously, drove his

Volkswagen Beetle cross-country to Seattle and started Cadabra, better known today as Amazon. The wrong job can hide your ideas and talents from the world and yourself. The resentment this breeds is understandable. And wasteful.

Freeing yourself from a job that slowly buries you can unleash enormous potential. Sociologist AnnaLee Saxenian discovered this while studying why Silicon Valley thrived and the East Coast technology sector in America floundered. The difference came down to organizational structure. East Coast companies, mainly around Boston's Route 128, emulated Washington DC's bureaucratic behemoths, constraining talent and ideas. In contrast, Silicon Valley nurtured a network of people and companies that moved between each other, competing or collaborating, rejuvenating the economic climate, and ensuring the rapid spread of ideas. This fluidity is why Silicon Valley, not the East Coast, is now synonymous with technology innovation.

RECOMBINING

If you cannot move, try moving the things you have before you to change perspective. Using what is in your hands instead of escaping from it can be a way of moving forward.

Jean-Luc De Meyer was a struggling Belgian musician who would make ends meet by working in an insurance firm. His band, Front 242, was influential in the budding electronic music scene in the 1980s but had limited commercial appeal. This would all change with the release of the song "Headhunter" in 1988. With a pulsating beat and bass, the song seems to be about a bounty hunter looking for his next victim. In reality, De Meyer had simply taken the sales strategy his boss used at the insurance firm: lock the target, bait the line, spread the net and catch the man. The song became a breakthrough hit for the band, and De Meyer could focus on music full time. Insurance sales strategy was the unlikely enabler and muse.

Neuroscientist David Eagleman, an expert on creativity, calls this kind of combing and mixing elements in new ways 'blending' and argues that it is one of the most common ways the brain generates new ideas. Examples range from the use of metaphors in language — William Shakespeare claiming that "all the world's a stage" — or fusion cuisine, like Peruvian Ceviche with its roots in South America and Japan — or inventions like Velcro, inspired by the blending of two unrelated observations: burrs sticking to a dog's fur and the need for a new type of fastener.

Another example of the power of new combinations, also from the field of electronic music, is the band Orchestral Manoeuvres in the Dark, or OMD for short. They had a couple of modest hit singles in the 1980s and early 1990s, like "If You Leave" and "Walking on the Milky Way." Even though they never had a number-one single, and while the hits started to dry up, their love of songwriting did not. They had a breakthrough idea when they performed on the same show where the Spice Girls had their debut televised performance. The all-male OMD, perceived as a dated 80s band — would write songs for girl bands instead, blending their songwriting talents with the budding superstars of the new millennium. Unfortunately, there were no takers. Nobody wanted or needed an OMD-penned song. Frustrated with the lack of interest, OMD took a radical step and created a female trio, auditioning over 30 singers for the project. Originally called Automatic Kitten because it sounded cool, family members of the singers kept mispronouncing the name, and they became Atomic Kitten. In 2001, their song "Whole Again" sold more than two million copies and topped the charts worldwide. It became OMD's first number-one single. Recombining songwriting skills with new singers created something better.

ESCAPIST DREAMS AND NIGHTMARES

The idea of escaping — whether from a job you detest or backing out of a career in decline — has romantic connotations. The stories described above have been selected because the outcomes were successful, which is not always true. The reason the word 'dare' is used is that escaping from one's reality can be a dangerous pursuit. It might lead to momentary freedom but can also result in long-term consequences like unfulfilled potential, lost opportunities and even physical harm.

The story of Christopher McCandless tragically illustrates the price of escape. He abandoned his possessions, gave his savings to charity, and ventured into the Alaskan wilderness, searching for what he thought would be 'a purer existence.' Unfortunately, his yearning led to his death. With little practical knowledge or experience of what living in the wild would entail, he ingested toxic wild plants and died of starvation. He was found in an old bus where he had been living. Losing your life is indeed the highest price to pay, but even lesser consequences may lead you to think twice about escaping from your current situation. Think of the disillusionment experienced by people who have left everything behind to join some utopian community or sect, only to find them fraught with problems, even abuse. Consider the loss of promising careers and relationships — the invisible opportunity cost — by those who impulsively quit jobs and responsibilities in search of something 'more meaningful.' As idealized visions brutally collide with reality, disillusionment and depression set in. Escaping from something places little or no value on what you have. It renders your current situation worthless, so it is not particularly brave to move elsewhere. For moving to be something you dare to do, you must know what you sacrifice. Put another way, it's only moving if you leave something of value behind. Otherwise, it's just quitting.

CONCLUSION: STAY INTERESTED AND INTERESTING

The French Nobel prize-winning author André Gide observed that we cannot discover new oceans without the courage to lose sight of the shore. The ability to move across oceans — once the privilege of a select few explorers — has become a dream within reach for most of us. It is also an economic necessity in an urbanizing world that runs on ideas. People like Justine Frischmann and Jeff Bezos illustrate the hidden potential in us that can be revealed by changing your job, locale or both. Yet moving should not primarily be seen as some success-boosting tool. And running away into the wilderness solves nothing for us and can even worsen the emotional burdens we carry. Moving is about rejuvenating your brain. Humans succumb to the habituation effect, wherein we become accustomed to a stimulus through repeated or prolonged exposure. The first kiss is usually very exciting. The millionth less so. Day one on vacation in a tropical paradise is magical. By day ten, you will have found things that annoy you and have grown tired of the breakfast buffet. The same goes for taste, views and ideas. As the philosopher Marcel Proust cynically put it: "If you want to avoid seeing someone, you should marry them."

By moving — going to new places, exploring new ideas, trying new ways — you become interested and interesting. If you do it often enough, you won't have to escape or quit your job. You might even find that new endeavours have enabled you to see your old situation in a new light.

If you want to compete, stay in existing structures and work harder to excel. Forward and up are the only things that matter.

If you want to create, take a step to the side. Or backward.

Dare to move.

SEVEN WAYS TO MOVE

1. **FREE YOURSELF FROM SHACKLES**
   If the place you are in hurts too much, it is time to readjust and move somewhere else.

2. **FIND A BETTER FIT!**
   Make a list of the places you think would fit you better. Visit them. Try living there for a short period to see if you are right.

3. **DON'T LEAVE EVERYTHING BEHIND!**
   Cutting chains is liberating, cutting roots is dangerous. Distinguish between the things that hold you down and the ones that ground you. Sometimes they are the same.

4. **MOVE YOUR MIND!**
   If you cannot move, change your perspective. Experiment with new ways. Play. You may have gotten stuck in a dead end, with a new world opening up just around the corner.

5. YOU ARE NOT THE ONLY ONE!

Take care of others who have moved. Your boring everyday existence is their new frontier. Help them discover it.

6. READ

It is the cheapest, most environmentally friendly way to travel.

7. DON'T DISAPPEAR

Wherever you go in the world, you will bring yourself along. Hiding from that fact will only bring misery. Find ways of enjoying your own company.

Experiment.

Try and fail while life seems eternal.

PART SIX

20+

DARE TO BE
TWENTYSOMETHING

When Jacqueline Gold was born, her father wept — not tears of joy, but disappointment. He had hoped for a son that could one day take over his business. This was the early 1960s, and women were still rare in the corporate world. Jacqueline was described as a "funny little child" raised in a home with material comforts but too little love and affection. Her mother kept her at home and away from friends. When Gold was 12, her mother started an affair with her father's best friend, often dumping the child in the garden, no matter the season, to wait outside while they did their business. The affair, predictably, led to a divorce, and the lover became Jacqueline Gold's stepfather. He was a creep who would subject her to sexual abuse and harassment.

She finally found the courage to tell him to stop in her mid-teens, which he did, but it understandably left an eternally bad aftertaste in Jacqueline regarding sexuality.

It would all change when she attended a Pippa Dee party in her early 20s. The parties, similar to the American Tupperware get-to-gethers, used a self-employed sales force of over 13,000 women to organize house party sales across the UK in the 1970s. She had a stroke of insight. What if she combined the Pippa Dee sales model with her father's business?

To call what her father did 'business' would be an overstatement. He had merely acquired four run-down sex shops. At that period, the shops catered solely to men, with blacked-out windows hiding an array of adult products. When Gold presented her idea for a revamp, one of the company's board members complained preposterously that women weren't interested in sex, questioning any need to broaden the business model.

The only person to stand up for her idea was her father, who gave her a loan to try out the idea.

She held a girls-only party to sell lingerie and, when the guests had settled in, sex toys. The atmosphere was nervous. But it worked.

She used the loan to advertise in newspapers and recruit more salespeople. More saleswomen, to be precise. The somewhat prude UK authorities viewed the activity as illegal and did their best to shut her down. She was arrested at a trade show. Job centres refused to carry her advertisements, and she was physically threatened when she opened a shop in Catholic Dublin. Yet the setbacks spurred her on. Slowly but surely, she built the brand Ann Summers into an empire. When she passed away in the early 2020s, there were more than 150 shops – 'pleasure emporiums' – all over the British Isles and Ireland. She had recruited over 13,000 saleswomen to host parties, and the turnover numbered hundreds of millions of pounds. She had not just taken over her father's business – she had radically transformed it. She had also helped champion a more feminine view of sex and sexuality and inspired millions of young women to feel that they, too, had a natural role as business leaders. In 2016, she was awarded the title of CBE, Commander of the British Empire, by the Queen for her services.

This section is about the opportunities we have and the challenges we face in our chiselling 20s. This time period is fertile ground for life-altering shifts as we move from the structure of childhood and education to a less-structured world of adult responsibilities, work and relationships. It is a time fraught with both danger and opportunity, where you have a chance to carve yourself into something unique.

THE TURBULENT 20s

The concept of 'teenagers,' as we understand it today, is largely a 20th-century invention, while modern ideas about childhood emerged in the 19th century. Before the Industrial Revolution, children were employed as labourers from a young age. However, with the advent of factories, child labour became impractical. Coinciding with this change, the concept of universal education for all children, not just those from wealthy families, came into legislation.

By the mid-20th century, increased longevity and radical changes in the workplace created ample time for leisure activities. For those navigating the years between childhood and full-fledged adulthood, a golden era emerged. Rebels, misfits, beatniks, hippies and punk rockers — all these subcultures were invented between 1950 and 1980 to suit the lifestyles of the young and restless. However, once individuals reached their early 20s, they were often considered responsible adults and left to manage their lives independently. For many, this transition was disastrous. Psychologists dubbed the age range between 20 and 29 the "forgotten developmental stage," a kind of quarter-life crisis where individuals were "starving for guidance on how to live in relation to their inner lives."

By the early 21st century, rates of mental health issues were rising, and the average age for the onset of depression had dropped from the early 50s to the mid-20s. A period once characterized by freedom and self-discovery had become torturous for many. One of the contributing factors was that many in their 20s attempted to emulate the adult lifestyles of their parents – securing a job, an apartment and a relationship – without considering if these choices were genuinely suitable for them. When setbacks like job loss or breakups occurred, they often felt isolated and despondent. The notion that one's 20s were the ideal time to solidify life commitments had become obsolete in a world with vastly different challenges and opportunities.

Individuals born in what is broadly termed the 'Western world' in 1948 could look forward to several decades of unbroken growth and opportunity. The French aptly named this period 'Les Trente Glorieuses,' or the 30 glorious years. In contrast, those born in 1998 faced years of turbulence, including financial crises, wars, pandemics, the threat of terrorism and looming climate disasters, along with the incessant chatter of social media.

Furthermore, the advice given to young people often fell into one of two categories: recycled 20th-century wisdom advocating independence and risk-taking, or stern manifestos preaching the value of discipline and subservience. By the 2020s, bookstores were overflowing with guides and rulebooks promising to steer 20-year-olds toward a more meaningful life, revealing the emotional and developmental void left between adolescence and adulthood.

The unsettled minds of twentysomethings had become political battlegrounds. Especially concerning were those individuals who, often taught to be skeptical of traditional beliefs, became susceptible to various ideologies, ready to believe in anything.

Yet, the reason life is so difficult to navigate in your 20s has other causes beyond a changing outer world. To find it, we need to look inside our bodies.

THE HALF-BAKED
BRAIN

Lena Dunham's pitch was different. The young New York filmmaker had written a memo to HBO executives with an idea for a new TV series. Normally, these pitches come from experienced producers with ideas that cross-fertilize two previously successful concepts: "It's like *Game of Thrones* but set in space" or "What if we make a show about a rich family like those in *Dallas* or *Dynasty* in the 1980s, but without a single likable character?" (This was the actual pitch for *Succession*.) Dunham's document was odd. It contained no plot, setting or even specific characters. Instead, she pointed to a developmental stage "between adolescence and adulthood," just after college, when "the shape of one's life is still raw and nebulous." "It's a period of flux," she wrote, that is "heartbreaking and hilarious," "humbling," "sexy," and "ripe for laughs." This "Facebook Generation," she continued, "is beautiful and maddening. They're self-aware and self-obsessed. They're my friends, and I've never seen them on TV."

The TV show she pitched, *Girls*, premiered in 2012 and became a cultural juggernaut, a commercial smash hit and Dunham's breakthrough hit. A different pitch that resonated with a mainstream audience.

Dunham perfectly describes the lost souls featured in this section, which begs the question: Why is life so 'raw and nebulous' at this stage? Beyond dramatic world changes, there is a more direct, biological reason people struggle in their 20s: their brain is simply not fully developed yet.

At the very front of the brain lies the prefrontal cortex, the last part to fully develop, usually in one's mid-20s. It plays a crucial role in making choices based on future consequences and is vital for inhibiting impulsive behaviour and delaying immediate gratification for long-term benefits. In other words, the absence of a fully functioning prefrontal cortex explains many of the woes facing 20-year-olds. When a global study examined age patterns in risk-taking worldwide, from China to the US, the riskiest behaviour was found at age 22. Yet the word 'risk' has two sides. It can refer to something with the potential to be destructive, but it can also describe a situation that is difficult to predict, where you are forced to take a chance on something or someone. The former is a bad risk; the latter has the potential to be a good kind. Lena Dunham daring to pitch to seasoned HBO executives was a good risk; she had little to lose beyond being ignored or declined. A 20-year-old experimenting with illegal drugs to feel better is a bad risk. The key, therefore, is to guide twentysomethings from bad to good risks, knowing that the slightly undeveloped brain is receptive to both kinds. The 20s should be the age of experimentation, a role once reserved for teenagers. This approach would also make stumbling blocks — like getting married too early or being fired from a job — much more forgiving. After all, what is experimentation but a series of planned failures?

MONOLITH
MOMENTS

In Arthur C. Clarke's *2001: A Space Odyssey*, a black marble block appears seemingly out of nowhere. The Monolith, as it's called, serves as a mysterious and enigmatic symbol that represents a guiding force in the evolution and progress of intelligent life. When Stanley Kubrick made a movie out of the book, the ape-like prehistoric creatures started using old bones as tools when they encountered the monolith. In the trailer for the movie *Barbie* in 2023, in homage to Stanley Kubrick's scene, young girls smashed up their old dolls when the iconic namesake appeared. The monolith — in its marble or plastic doll form — catalyzes evolution.

The Pippa Dee meeting Jaqueline Gold attended at the age of 21 served as her monolith. Jane Goodall worked as a secretary in Kenya when she was exposed to studying chimpanzees as a research assistant. She was 26, and it became a lifelong obsession. Gerard Way, a 24-year-old cartoonist in New York, realized when he watched the Twin Towers tragically crumble on September 11, 2001, that he needed to do something with his life. He founded the band My Chemical Romance, which became a soundtrack for and voice of disillusioned adolescents worldwide. Hiroshi Mikitani was 29 and worked as a banker when an earthquake devastated his hometown, Kobe. He wanted to help rebuild and revitalize the economy, far from the banking sector. He founded Rakuten, which became one of Japans best known digital companies.

Gabriel García Márquez was in his early 20s studying law in Bogota when he read Franz Kafka's *The Metamorphosis*. It reminded him of the stories his grandmother told him as a child, where magical elements lived alongside normal, everyday events. It led him to craft his genre, magical realism, for which he would later win a Nobel Prize in literature.

When the coin drops, things click into place, and new patterns emerge, it's a 'monolith moment.' It can most certainly happen to you at any point in your life. Still, they mean the most in your 20s because you are stranded between the passivity and wonder you feel as a child — being an observer of the adult world — and the entrenched mindset of the fully formed adult, where you have an established framework unsuitable for new adventures.

What the chance encounters of Gold, Goodall, Way, Mikitani and Márquez reveal is not only the inspirational power of these meetings but also the futility of dreams as a catalyst. Most career advice passed on from generation to generation will feature a variation of 'follow your dreams.' But with the prefrontal cortex — and its ability to predict future outcomes — not fully formed, dreams are bound to fall short of reality. A monolith moment is a reactive way to meet the future; you let reality surprise you. You expose yourself to happy accidents and realize that wonderful things hide behind uncomfortable risks.

THE RESOURCE CURSE

"[Abraham] Lincoln is the leanest, lankest, most ungainly mass of legs, arms and hatchet-face ever strung upon a single frame. He has most unwarrantably abused the privilege that all politicians have of being ugly." These were the words of a political journalist to describe the man who would run for president in 1860. He was not alone in thinking Abraham Lincoln was ugly. Even an 11-year-old girl writing him a fan letter felt the need to add, "If you let your whiskers grow [...] you would look a great deal better for your face is so thin." He did eventually grow a beard but was constantly aware of his less-than-favourable looks. In a specific interaction with a woman, she eyed Lincoln and said, "Jeepers, Mr President, you are one homely looking fellow." Lincoln answered, "Yes, ma'am, I know, but I cannot help it, that is how God made me."

Lincoln's face was just one of many disadvantages life had dealt him. His first career in business failed, as did his first attempt to run for office in the Illinois General Assembly in the 1830s. This was just before Ann Rutledge, his first love, passed away, a devastating personal loss. All throughout his 20s and 30s, he had serious bouts of depression, or melancholia, as it was called at the time. To say nothing about how his life ended, of course.

Yet Lincoln is known as one of America's most admired and respected presidents. He persevered and worked his way up as a lawyer, transitioned into politics and, when he became president, championed the abolition of slavery. His Gettysburg Address is still considered one of the most impactful speeches ever, observing that the United States was "conceived in Liberty, and dedicated to the proposition that all men are created equal."

The question is whether Lincoln's disadvantages were actually to his advantage.

In macroeconomics, there is something called the 'resource curse.' It is an economic paradox wherein countries or regions abundant in natural resources, such as minerals, oil or gas, often fail to experience proportional economic growth or development and may even suffer from negative social, political and economic outcomes. In short, countries born rich don't try as hard. Some of the most successful economic experiments in the world happened in places that had absolutely nothing going for them, with Dubai and Las Vegas stuck in the middle of deserts and Singapore perched at the end of a swamp.

This can be applied to people. Attractiveness bias is a psychological phenomenon wherein people tend to favour those who are physically attractive, often attributing positive qualities like intelligence and trustworthiness to them without concrete evidence. This bias can impact various areas of life, such as employment, social interactions and legal outcomes.

Similarly, tall people are overrepresented in leadership roles.

In short, positive physical endowments often give you a free ride. Yet this blessing might be a curse if you fall short of your potential. Furthermore, people who have already paid a social price — such as ugliness — tend to be better at promoting new ideas, just like Lincoln.

Or think of incompetence and the number of successful companies — like Virgin Records or Apple — started by inexperienced outsiders. As Bob Pittman, the founder of MTV, a radically new TV channel in the early 1980s, once remarked: "The only reason we created MTV is that we did not realize we could not do it." Naivety and audacity reach further than good looks and executive titles.

If the turbulent 20s are to become an age of experimentation, struggling with your shortcomings, though painful, is a friend, not an adversary.

CONCLUSION: THE COCOON YEARS

Being young is about being on the outside looking in. What is the adult world really like? What seems to make people happy, angry or sad? Is anybody in there just like me, or am I alone? Just like trying on a new pair of jeans, you squeeze your legs through and then pull them up, hoping that they will fit. Sometimes they do. Often they don't. The same goes for lifestyles. You start trying to live a certain way in your 20s — often copying what your peers or parents did. This is known as 'pretend adulthood' and often ends with things falling apart and a profound loneliness.

You try, fail and try again. You are no longer a caterpillar and not yet a butterfly, but a cocoon. And just like there is no linear, predictable relationship between what a caterpillar, a cocoon and a butterfly look like, predicting where you will be and who you will become is impossible. Abraham Lincoln was a failed entrepreneur in his 20s and Jaqueline Gold was considered a menace to British society. The cocoon years are a roller coaster between crises where you recalibrate plans, explore new things and reinvent yourself. It is an age of experimentation. This mindset has been adopted for romance, with dating being an acceptable social interaction to find love and sex. It is applied experimentation. We need to find that experimental mindset for everything that matters in life and it starts in your 20s.

If you want to compete, exploit only the things you are good at, dream big and ensure you look good. Plan extensively.

If you want to create, dare to stay a little longer in uncomfortable things. Be ugly — in a literal or figurative sense — experiment and be prepared to fail.

Dare to be twentysomething.

SEVEN WAYS TO BE TWENTYSOMETHING

1. LIVE IN THE LIMINAL
   Liminal is a fancy word that describes a situation, phase or feeling of being in between things. Imagine you're playing a video game and have just completed a tough level, but you haven't yet moved onto the next level — you're on the loading screen. You're not in the past level any more, but you're not yet in the next one, either. That's a liminal space. You're sort of in a transitional phase.

2. REWARDS REQUIRE RISKS
   Take risks to find wonderful things, but be prepared to fail.

3. DON'T SEE ANYTHING AS FINITE
   You are in development and transition. Everything you do, make and try in these years will pass. Don't make irrevocable decisions.

4. FIND ALLIED MISFITS

They are bound to be scattered, so like the drunkard in the famous parable, don't just look under the street light because the light is better there.

5. EVOLVE, DON'T REVOLT

Anger is fuel, not a building material. Let yourself evolve further, don't pivot and run in completely different directions.

6. ACCEPT THAT MANY HAVE A HARD TIME TAKING YOU SERIOUSLY

Everyone was young once. We tend to be unforgiving to the people we once were and take it out on new generations.

7. SLOW CHANGE IS THE KEY

Change what you don't like about yourself but let it take time.

Evolve.

Become who you were meant to be.

PART SEVEN

DARE TO
GET OLDER

Dietrich Mateschitz was probably tired on that fateful day in Hong Kong. The Austrian travelled the world selling German toothpaste, and jet lag tends to hit particularly hard when you travel from West to East. His Asian counterparts, two brothers of Thai origin, offered him a concoction called Krating Daeng. Roughly translated as 'Red Gaur,' named after a type of cattle common in Southeast Asia, the drink was seen as a kind of legal miracle drug. It consisted of guarana, taurine, caffeine, sucrose and ginseng; Mateschitz found it worked wonders for his fatigue. He formed a new partnership with the Thai brothers, carbonated the drink to suit European palates, and began selling it in Austria as 'Red Bull' in 1987. So far, this story resembles many anecdotes about how companies were built and fortunes were made. Mark Zuckerberg started a website to rate people's attractiveness before pivoting to what was initially called 'The Facebook.' Steve Jobs founded Apple in a garage, dreaming of turning computers into 'bicycles for the mind.' Oprah Winfrey rebounded from being fired as a television newsreader to start her own talk show. However, unlike these figures who were in their 20s, Dierich Mateschitz was twice as old when he created Red Bull. This section is about how you can grow to be innovative and make a meaningful difference as you age.

TIME,
THE GREAT SHAPER

Modern culture is fixated on youth. From South Korea to Southern California, pop groups, movies, fashion magazines and sports teams predominantly feature individuals between the ages of 18 and 25. This age range has also been the most lucrative target for marketers for the past 50 or so years. Indeed, youth seems to be a prerequisite if one wishes to make a significant impact in either athletics or pop music. The average age of world-record holders in sports is around 24, while pop stars often create their most impactful work around the age of 27. Elvis Presley was just 19 when he created "The Sun Sessions," and Marvin Gaye was 32 when he released "What's Going On."

Age and achievement often intertwine in fascinating ways across human endeavours. Take mathematics, for example. The Fibonacci sequence was discovered by Leonardo Pisano in his book *Liber Abaci* at 32, a prime age for many in this discipline.

In the realm of physics, breakthroughs also tend to come early. Marie Curie was just 31 when she conducted her pioneering research, and Einstein was a mere 36 during his annus mirabilis.

But exploration seems to favour a slightly more seasoned individual. Francis Drake and Roald Amundsen set their marks on history at 39 with their epic journeys around the globe and to the pole.

Shifting to more creative fields, the narrative changes. Innovation, philosophy, literature, art and architecture often benefit from the wisdom of 40-plus years. Frank Lloyd Wright crafted *Fallingwater*, his masterpiece, at 68. Picasso painted the iconic *Guernica* at 56. Meanwhile, Rembrandt and Monet produced their most prized works well into their 50s and 60s.

In literature, maturity seems key. Gertrude Stein, at 59, gave us *The Autobiography of Alice B. Toklas*. Margaret Atwood was 46 when *The Handmaid's Tale* came out. J.R.R. Tolkien, Joseph Conrad and Virginia Woolf all crossed into their 40s before publishing their first novels. On average, authors might spend a dozen to 15 years before their book hits the shelves. This time isn't wasted; it's dedicated to refining their craft and deepening their worldview.

John Danenbarger, a literary expert, notes the importance of life experience in writing. Conrad's seafaring days profoundly influenced his *Heart of Darkness*, and John le Carré's espionage work lent authenticity to his *Smiley* novels. It seems clear: time invested in living and learning is essential for depth and authenticity in one's work.

Time, it appears, is the secret ingredient. To prepare and perfect one's art, there is no substitute for the years spent amassing experience and honing skills.

The business world is especially accommodating to older age. Harland D. Sanders was in his 60s when he opened his first Kentucky Fried Chicken restaurant and Ray Kroc was a milkshake machine salesman in his 50s when he discovered the McDonald Brothers' restaurant in Pasadena. Warren Buffett, the famous investor, made over 95% of his fortune after his 65th birthday. The fashion designer Vera Wang, like Joseph Conrad and John Le Carré in literature, spent nearly two decades in fashion journalism, calibrating her unique eye for style. This was after she had spent her teenage years and early 20s being a figure skater but failed to make the US Olympics Team. The reason has to do with risk-taking. While the half-baked brain of people in their early 20s tends to steer them toward dangerous activities, like adrenaline sports, or downright stupid endeavours, like driving drunk, positive risk-taking peaks in middle adulthood, between 40 and 65. Meeting new people, making new connections, and seeing fragments you've encountered fall into place into a new, complete picture are just some of these positive risks. Finding your voice in literature or sharpening your business acumen is like a boiling stew — it will taste better the longer it cooks.

THE PREPARED SPIRIT

When you are young, your mind is mercurial — sparkling between ideas, fields of interest or whatever happens to capture your attention at some precise moment. This is known as fluid intelligence, the cognitive ability to solve problems quickly. Advertising agencies tend to be staffed with twentysomethings ready to apply their fast-paced minds to brand strategies and sales tactics.

Similarly, armies consist mainly of young people — often male — who forego any deeper analysis to quickly invade enemy head-quarters, solving problems that arise in real time. Computer games, in all their fast-paced complexity, also tend to be a domain for the young.

As you age, fluid intelligence plateaus and declines, but you gain crystallized intelligence — the accumulated knowledge you can recall and apply as needed. Designing a house or writing a book are two endeavours that benefit from a large pile of cumulative knowledge. Ray Kroc, Dietrich Mateschitz and Vera Wang had accumulated enough knowledge in sales and marketing to discern which ideas had potential and which did not. Unlike fluid intelligence, crystallized intelligence doesn't necessarily slow down with age. On the contrary, fed with curiosity, it can grow for a long time.

Pitting these two cognitive concepts against each other, however, does them a disservice. Oftentimes, both kinds are needed to gain new insights. Take the German chemist August Kekulé as an example. He started working in his early 20s to understand how chemicals bonded together. In particular, he wanted to comprehend and map the structure of benzene, an aromatic compound. The answer would take 20 years and finally came to him in a dream when he was in his late 30s. In this dream, Kekulé envisioned a snake swallowing its tail. All the pieces he had gathered fell into place, and the circular benzene ring was born. Experience and fluid insight came together serendipitously in a dream. Some might call it luck, but Kekulé would simply shrug and say that "visions come to prepared spirits."

Another prepared spirit was Professor Hans Rosling, who for decades travelled and lectured to medical undergraduates about public health and how it varied across continents. He was especially frustrated by his academically gifted students, many of whom seemed to hold outdated views of Africa that were stuck in the 1960s — when the continent was often seen as uniformly poor and backward, with low life expectancy. He grappled with various pedagogical tools for many years. In 2005, at 57 years old, he collaborated with his son and daughter-in-law, both in their 30s, to transform his dry statistical data into a graphics-driven interface illustrating progress on many dimensions. In 2006, his TED talk, "The Best Stats You've Ever Seen," gained worldwide attention. The following year, the company he had established with his family was acquired by Google. Luck had favoured the blend of prepared and agile minds.

LEARNING FOR YOURSELF

George Clooney was in his mid-30s when his acting career took a significant upward turn. Known for his role in *ER*, a long-running medical drama that delved into the lives of emergency room staff in a Chicago hospital, Clooney played the compassionate yet slightly rebellious main character, Dr Ross. The show was produced by Steven Spielberg. At one point, after the show had been on the air for a few seasons, Spielberg tapped the monitor displaying the camera feed and said to Clooney, "If you stop moving your head around, you'll be a movie star." If you compare Clooney's acting in *ER* to the movie roles he later assumed, a stunning difference emerges. As a movie star, Clooney exhibited a more constrained, calm presence and seldom moved his head.

The point of this anecdote is twofold: it illustrates not only how a minor adjustment can make a substantial difference — particularly if one is as photogenic as Clooney — but also how impactful a piece of advice can be. Sadly, wisdom that could easily be transferred from the elderly to the young, preventing redundant mistakes, is disregarded. Author Adam Mastroianni learned this lesson the hard way when he attempted to dissuade young graduate students from attending Oxford University. Despite his miserable experience at the prestigious institution — where he found both the education and professors lacking and an atmosphere of isolation and alienation pervasive — his warnings fell on deaf ears. Students returned a year later with predictable complaints mirroring Mastroianni's own.

In exploring this phenomenon, Mastroianni discovered that people have an inherent need to seek meaning on their own. Amidst the endless stream of daily information, insights and factoids, arranging this chaos into a meaningful pattern is a uniquely individual endeavour. What resonates with one person may not matter to the next. This personal crafting of narratives gives us a kind of immunity to the experiences of others. Even if we listen, we may not fully understand someone else's journey, no matter how frequently they share it. As a result, a persistent disconnect exists between the fluid minds of the young and the crystallized wisdom of the elderly.

Wisdom is the recovery of innocence at the far end of experience, as a wise man once said.

CONCLUSION: THE HIDDEN HORIZON

"Old age isn't a battle; old age is a massacre." These dystopian words are spoken in Philip Roth's novel *Everyman*. There are things to worry about in growing old and the end looks the same for all of us. Yet, there are also some underappreciated aspects of ageing. Research has shown that people become increasingly unhappy up until the age of 47. The U-shaped happiness curve shows how our emotional wellbeing starts to drop off in our late teens and early 20s and doesn't return to a high level until we are in our mid-60s. Although happiness is a tremendously fuzzy concept to measure, there may be practical reasons our self-reported happiness declines. Professor David Blanchflower studied hundreds of thousands of people in over a hundred countries. He could rule out the influence of wealth and, once certain basic conditions were met, other socioeconomic factors, as the results looked highly similar across most countries. What he did find was that once the exuberant dreams of the young meet the practical demands of reality, a decline in happiness starts, and it does not let up until you let go of these lost horizons and broken dreams. Letting go tends to happen around the age of 47. And 73 days to use the exact statistical findings. The happiness curve reveals that we live two very different kinds of lives. One is built on omnipotence, big dreams and the quick minds of the young. The other starts when we accept life's imperfections and apply what we have learned, what people we have met, and the ideas we have encountered. David Bowie once called ageing an extraordinary process where you become the person you always should have been. It is a new beginning, a second chance. Yet, as filmmaker Orson Welles remarked, "Being alive means not killing the tensions one carries within oneself. On the contrary, a poet must seek out and cultivate his contradictions." Ageing is about striking a balance between the fluid and the crystallized.

Dare to get older is a strange thing to advise. Time has only one direction — forward — and its effect on our minds and bodies happens automatically, if not evenly or fairly. Dare to get older means leaning into the positive effects of ageing, embracing its features and discovering who you are meant to be.

Ageing also resolves the Gretchen Question posed in the Introduction. When you are young and eager, you tend to compete. You compare yourself to others and try to climb a ladder to reach the top in whatever field you conquer — zero-sum games with winners and losers.

Somewhere in your life, you will fail. You fall off the ladder or you are kicked off. You may fall ill, get divorced, get fired and see all your dreams burn out.

You suffer.

Time goes by.

Your focus shifts to discovery and creation.

You find new roads and new ways.

You find a new horizon hidden behind the lost one.

Do you want to compete and be better?

Or do you want to create and be different?

Time is on your side.
Dare to get older.

"

Beyond mountains, there are mountains.

Haitian proverb

SEVEN WAYS TO GET OLDER

1. ### LET GO LIGHTLY
   Don't hold on to things you can no longer carry or hold. Accept that age changes some things for the worse.

2. ### TAKE GREATER RISKS
   You might have held back too long in life. Now is the time to let it rip.

3. ### SEND THE ELEVATOR BACK DOWN
   Give chances to new people in your field, like others once helped you.

4. ### ABANDON ENTRENCHED POSITIONS
   The world keeps evolving, and so should you. If something is especially shocking or provocative to you, it is a sign that you are learning.

5. ### PACKAGE YOUR WISDOM AS TREATS
   Make them funny and self-deprecating. It helps the rest of us digest it more easily.

6. PLAN FOR THE INFINITE
   Just because your years may be numbered doesn't mean your dreams have to be.

7. AND MAKE YOUR DREAMS A MIX OF THE BIG AND SMALL
   Going to the moon isn't necessarily better than a cold beer on the beach. Just less attainable.

Embark
Embrace
Enlighten
Elevate
Experiment
Evolve

PART EIGHT

CONCLUSION: BEING THE DIFFERENCE

In the early 2020s, fans sent Nick Cave, an Australian singer-song-writer, lyrics composed by AI "in the style of Nick Cave." Known for elegiac melodies and deep lyrics about love, loss and the pain of living, Cave would have none of it.

"This song sucks," he said, responding to what one fan sent in (the chorus: "I am the sinner, I am the saint, I am the darkness, I am the light, I am the hunter, I am the prey, I am the devil, I am the saviour.") "Songs arise out of suffering," he continued. "They are predicated upon the complex, internal human struggle of creation ... data doesn't suffer. ChatGPT has no inner being; it has been no-where, it has endured nothing, it has not had the audacity to reach beyond its limitations, and hence it doesn't have the capacity for a shared transcendent experience, as it has no limitations from which to transcend ... writing a good song is not mimicry or replication or pastiche, it is the opposite. It is an act of self-murder that destroys all one has strived to produce in the past."

Part of being human is to suffer. To be different is to suffer even more. AI offers to bypass the suffering and produce ideas at speed. We should not heed its call. While technology can simplify and speed things up, we also lose great benefits. In the grinding cogs of the sameness machine, we lose what sets us apart as individuals: the hurt, the pain and the struggle that enable us to make some-thing different. To make a difference.

AI is a replication machine; it copies what is already there.

You and I, on the other hand, are unique. We have a chance to see things in ways that nobody has before. We can create something nobody else has thought or even dreamt about.

You are a source. Your stories, your scars, your triumphs and your tragedies all contribute to making you who you are. They contribute to what you see in the world and how you see it. They influence what you do and make. You can share your source with the rest of us — poetry, music, business, ideas, writing or just being you. You are the custodian of something unique.

As the music producer Rick Rubin puts it: "We perceive, filter and collect data, then curate an experience for ourselves and others based on this information set. Whether we do this consciously or unconsciously, by being alive, we are active participants in the ongoing process of creation."

BEYOND (L)IMITATIONS

Take a moment to browse the seven-point lists at the end of each section. From the first — write! — to the last — making your dreams a mix of the big and small. What they all have in common is courage. Not the kind of kamikaze instinct that makes people bungee jump or eat chilli peppers with outrageously high Scoville scores, but the kind of courage that enables us to have an honest conversation with ourselves. Who am I? Deep down, below appearances, accomplishments, fleeting thoughts and feelings.

This book has been an attempt to illuminate the intricate web of what makes us different as human beings. Whether it's our experiences, our inherited traits — or unfortunate mutations thereof — or what we set out to do in life. It has shown that the answer floats somewhere in between these elements.

There are approximately eight billion people alive on Earth today. If you are one in a million — once the expression used to denote uniqueness — it means there are over 8,000 of you alive today. We are constantly bombarded with facts and opinions about how deeply problematic this abundance of human life has become, from overcrowding to overconsumption.

Thomas Malthus, an 18th-century economist, believed that humanity's flourishing would be its death knell — with food, water and other resources too scarce to last beyond the mere billion people alive at the time. Humans are a burden.

A hundred years later, the Danish economist Ester Boserup would propose a radically different theory. More people do not use up resources, she argued; they ensure that we find new ways to produce food and increase the yield. More people ensure more human brains to solve new problems. Humans are a gift.

The difference between a Malthusian and a Boserupian perspective will fundamentally shape how you view our modern world and its prospects.

If humans are a burden, life is a race against time. A jigsaw puzzle to complete as fast as possible. A hierarchy to master. A competition to win. Us and them. Winners and losers. Insiders and outsiders.

If humans are a gift, what we will be able to create is a mystery. What we carry within us, and what we make of it, is unique.

The best idea society has for its young today is to get them to copy — in school, university and beyond. Children who stray too far from this are singled out, labelled, medically diagnosed and bullied by their peers. It is unworthy of a world that seeks progress, innovation and creativity.

You cannot expect a flock of well-behaved clones — fit-ins instead of misfits — to invent anything remotely original. You cannot expect a world that treats differences as a handicap to undergo any meaningful change. Problems, injustices and ignorance will be shovelled from one generation to the next. A grey, repetitive future replaces the shimmering dawn of a new tomorrow.

Yet there is another way.

You don't have to learn a language by reciting sentences and repeating them on an exam. You can travel to faraway places and try to find your way around by learning new words.

You don't have to copy your way to success; you can create your way into and out of the unknown.

Maya Angelou teaches us to dig deep into the hidden chasms of ourselves.

Temple Grandin shows us that your differences are a lens to see through, not a wall to isolate you.

Jan Boklöv is a peacock; when he flew, he did it differently, despite what others said.

Franz Jägerstätter's life teaches us about thinking and believing in the greater, long-term good.

Justine Frischmann shows us that leaving it all behind and taking a leap of faith can land us in a better place.

Jaqueline Gold took a risk at a young age.

Dietrich Mateschitz waited until his 40s before he took that risk.

Courage is in shorter supply than genius. Yet these people are not alone. Every day, somebody somewhere takes the first step on a path never before travelled. And just imagine all the unwritten stories. The billions as of yet unborn, who will someday make their mark in the world, big or small.

Getting people to seek out and emphasize what makes them different is key to breaking out of the repetitive cycle and onto a path of progress. The world needs more rebels, misfits and troublemakers to solve grand challenges or just invent a better kind of traffic light.

This is why we should dream of a world where differences are not just accepted and tolerated but celebrated.

THE OPPOSITE OF SUCCESS

We tend to see quality as a linear spectrum where an A is success and F is a failure. On that line, we avoid extremes, especially anything near an F. The result is that we often land somewhere in the middle, like a B- or C+. What the stories shared in this book try to convey is that quality is circular, not linear. The F is next door to an A. Lena Dunham's pitch for *Girls* could easily have been a warning for how not to pitch a TV show. Krating Daeng — the origin for Red Bull — could easily have been a flop. Jan Boklöv could have crashed on his first attempt at ski jumping differently and the V-style would have been forgotten. Ignaz Semmelweiss pushed on with his idea about hygiene even though he had an entire profession against him. And so on.

It is only when we find courage and take a leap of faith into the unknown that we can discover new dimensions. To be different — thinking, doing and dreaming differently — is to expose yourself to discomfort.

The shame of being wrong.

The pain of failure.

The noise of ridicule.

It is also the only way to bring humanity forward. It is the price of progress.

GO ON
AND DEVIATE

Our time in this life is short. It has, on average, a little over 4,000 weeks. How you spend those weeks is how you spend your life. Don't hide away from the world. Don't sit alone in guilt and shame. Explore the depths of yourself. Embrace the pain. Enhance and express your individuality. Embark on new adventures. Evolve.

Meaning is not something you get; it is something you give. Infuse things with meaning. Elevate the hidden, forgotten and ignored parts of yourself. Make sure you make your own meaning, don't copy someone else's. Meet yourself. Love yourself. Fall in love with solitude.

Remember that your biochemical and experiential components are unique.

FOLLOW THE SOURCE.

GO TO WHERE IT LEADS YOU.

DARE TO DIFFER.

DARE TO MAKE A DIFFERENCE.

DARE TO BE DIFFERENT.

SOURCES

The epigraphs quote is from
Auden, W.H. and Kronenberger, Louis (1966). *The Viking Book of Aphorisms*. New York: Viking Press.

INTRODUCTION: MAKING THE DIFFERENCE

The Goldman Sachs study of AI is from
"Generative AI could raise global GDP by 7%." Goldman Sachs. https://www.goldmansachs.com/intelligence/pages/generative-ai-could-raise-global-gdp-by-7-percent.html

Søren Kierkegaard's thoughts on anxiety are from
Kierkegaard, S. (2015). *The Concept of Anxiety*. (A. Hannay, Trans.). Princeton University Press.

THE STRUCTURE OF THIS BOOK: SEVEN DARES — SEVEN RUBICONS TO CROSS

The George Miller paper referred to is
Miller, G. A. (1956). "The magical number seven, plus or minus two: Some limits on our capacity for processing information." *Psychological Review*. 63 (2): 81–97. CiteSeerX 10.1.1.308.8071.

PART ONE: DARE TO DIG DEEP

The story of Maya Angelou is from
Wagner-Martin, L. (2021). *The Life of the Author: Maya Angelou*. Wiley-Blackwell.

The first quote is from
NPR. (28 May, 2014). "'Fresh Air' remembers poet and memoirist Maya Angelou." Retrieved from https://www.npr.org/2014/05/28/316707321/fresh-air-remembers-poet-and-memoirist-maya-angelou
Retrieved on 14 August, 2023.

The second quote is from
"Maya Angelou: I Know Why the Caged Bird Sings." World Book Club. BBC World Service. October 2005. Retrieved on 17 August, 2023.

The third quote is from
Angelou, M. (1969). *I Know Why the Caged Bird Sings*. Random House.

The Haruki Murakami quote is from
Murakami, H. (2000). *Norwegian Wood*. Vintage.

The Peter Thiel quote is from
Thiel, P. and Masters, B. (2014). *Zero to One: Notes on Startups, or How to Build the Future*.
Crown Business.

The Gregory Treverton quote is from
Farnam Street. (n.d.). "What's the difference between a puzzle and a mystery?"
Retrieved from https://fs.blog/whats-the-difference-between-a-puzzle-and-a-mystery/

The Eric Weinstein quote is from
Triggernometry. (2023). "Eric Weinstein — All hell is about to break loose." *YouTube*. https://
www.youtube.com/watch?v=DzHYIolSb3w

The Joan Didion quote is from
Didion, J. (1968). *Slouching Towards Bethlehem*. Farrar, Straus & Giroux.

PART TWO: DARE TO BE AN OUTSIDER

The story of Temple Grandin is from
Grandin, T. (2010). *Thinking in Pictures, Expanded Edition: My Life with Autism*. Vintage.

The quote is from
Keltner. D. (3 April, 2023). "Temple Grandin shares her journey with autism."
Greater Good Magazine. https://greatergood.berkeley.edu/article/item/
temple_grandin_shares_her_journey_with_autism

The statement about ancestors and group survival is from
Dunbar, R. (1996). *Grooming, Gossip, and the Evolution of Language*.
Harvard University Press.

The statement about brain reward and conformity is from
Berns, G. S. et al. (2010). "Neural mechanisms of the influence of popularity on adolescent
ratings of music." *NeuroImage*, 49(3), 2687-2696.

The statement about anterior cingulate cortex and deviation from norms is from
Eisenberger, N. I. (2012). "The pain of social disconnection: Examining the shared neural
underpinnings of physical and social pain." *Nature Reviews Neuroscience*, 13(6), 421-434.

The statement about mirror neurons and empathy is from
Rizzolatti, G. & Craighero, L. (2004). "The mirror-neuron system." *Annual Review of
Neuroscience*, 27, 169-192.

Erving Goffman's theory is from
SparkNotes Editors. Section2. "In identity and reality." *SparkNotes LLC*.
https://www.sparknotes.com/sociology/identity-and-reality/section2/

The quote from *Billions* is from
Tobias, S. (24 February, 2017. "Billions' season 2, episode 2: Nifty shades of Weiner."
New York Times. https://www.nytimes.com/2017/02/24/arts/television/billions-season-2-episode-2-recap.html

The BBC Study is described here
"Are dyslexia and wealth linked? Study finds individuals with dyslexia more
likely to be millionaires." *LD Online*. https://www.ldonline.org/ld-topics/
self-esteem-stress-management/are-dyslexia-and-wealth-linked-study-finds-individuals

Richard Branson calling dyslexia a superpower can be found here
"Sir Richard Branson opens up on his secret superpower dyslexia." *YouTube*, uploaded by
This Morning, 27 April, 2023, https://youtu.be/QrbVoBqlxaY

The study about ADHD being an evolutionary mismatch can be found here
Swanepoel, A. et al. (2017). "How evolutionary thinking can help us to understand ADHD."
BJPsych Advances, 23(6), 410-418. doi:10.1192/apt.bp.116.016659

The story about Bob Geldof and the quotes are from
Duerden, N. (2022). *Exit Stage Left: The Curious Afterlife of Pop Stars*. Headline Publishing.

Thomas Kuhn's research is summarized in
Kuhn, T. S. (1962). *The Structure of Scientific Revolutions*. University of Chicago Press.

The Charles Bukowski quote is from
Bukowski, C. (2003). *Sunlight Here I Am: Interviews and Encounters, 1963-1993*.
Sun Dog Press.

The William Blake quote was written on the wall of the William Blake exhibition at
Tate Britain in 2019.

Adam Grant's idea about groups can be found here
Grant, A. (2021). *Think Again: The Power of Knowing What You Don't Know*. Viking.

The isolation effect is described here
Chakraborty, A. (30 September, 2017). "The isolation effect: Why we notice the red tomato,
and ignore all the green ones." *Medium*. https://medium.com/@coffeeandjunk/
design-psychology-isolation-effect-a54e5b3dca0

PART THREE: DARE TO SUFFER

The story of Jan Boklöv is from an exhibition at Norrbottens Museum.
Online resource: https://www.ushnorrbotten.se/sv/fodelse/
jan-boklov-uppfinnaren-av-v-stilen/
Translated by the author.

The research on athletes and mental health can be found here
Z.A. Poucher et al. "Prevalence of symptoms of common mental disorders among elite
Canadian athletes," *Psychology of Sport and Exercise*, Volume 57, 2021, 102018.

The video of Michael Richards's outburst can be seen here
"Michael Richards goes crazy." (20 November, 2006). [Video file]. Retrieved from
https://www.youtube.com/watch?v=amjUNF_R_PY

The quote from Lol Tolhurst is from
Tolhurst, L. (2016). *Cured: The Tale of Two Imaginary Boys*. Da Capo Press.

The Friedrich Nietzsche quote is from
Nietzsche, F. (2017). *Thus Spoke Zarathustra*. CreateSpace Independent Publishing Platform.

The story of Dustin Hoffman and Sir Laurence Olivier can be found here
Simkins, M. (31 March, 2016). "Method acting can go too far – just ask Dustin
Hoffman." *The Guardian*: https://www.theguardian.com/commentisfree/2016/mar/31/
method-acting-dustin-hoffman-meryl-streep

The story of Trent Reznor can be found here
NPR Staff. 2011. "Trent Reznor: The Fresh Air interview." *NPR*. 19 December, 2011.
https://www.npr.org/2011/12/19/143834396/trent-reznor-the-fresh-air-interview

The story of The Edge playing guitar on "Love is Blindness" is from
Guggenheim, D. (Director). (2011). *From the Sky Down* [Film]. Universal Music.

The Blaise Pascal quote is from
Pascal, B. (1995). *Pensées*. Penguin Classics.

The Pew Study referred to can be found here
Smith, A. 2015. "Chapter three: A week in the life analysis of smartphone users."
Pew Research Center: Internet & Technology. 1 April, 2015. https://www.pewresearch.org/
internet/2015/04/01/chapter-three-a-week-in-the-life-analysis-of-smartphone-users/

The Simpsons episode referenced is
"HOMR." *Wikipedia*. https://en.wikipedia.org/wiki/HOMR

Tennessee Williams's essay and the quote from it can be found here
Williams, T. (30 November, 1947). "On a Streetcar named success; Tennessee Williams on a streetcar named success." *New York Times:* https://www.nytimes.com/1947/11/30/archives/on-a-streetcar-named-success-tennessee-williams-on-a-streetcar.html

PART FOUR: DARE TO BE KIND

The story of Franz Jägerstätter is from
Zahn, G. (1986). *In Solitary Witness. The Life and Death of Franz Jägerstätter* (Revised ed.). Springfield, Illinois: Templegate Publishers.

The Mary Karr quote is from
Karr, M. (2005). *The Liars' Club: A Memoir*. Penguin Books.

The neuroscience experiment is described in detail and taken from
McRaney, D. (2023). *How Minds Change: The New Science of Belief, Opinion and Persuasion*. Oneworld Publications.

The story of Tony Robbins is taken from
SunInMe.org. (n.d.). "The true story of Tony Robbins." Retrieved from https://suninme.org/true-story/tony-robbins

PART FIVE: DARE TO MOVE

The story of Justine Frischmann is from
Needham, A. (14 March, 2016). "Justine Frischmann: Waking Up from Elastica to Art in America." *The Guardian*. https://www.theguardian.com/artanddesign/2016/mar/14/justine-frischmann-elastica-interview-volta-art-fair

And
Anonymous. (n.d.). "Justine Frischmann: Snapping Back." *The Times*. https://www.thetimes.co.uk/article/justine-frischmann-elastica-qjvp8nkg6

The statistic about popstar life expectancy is from
Bellis, M. et al (19 December, 2012) "Dying to be famous: retrospective cohort study of rock and pop star mortality and its association with adverse childhood experiences," *British Medical Journal*.

The shift from a hunter-gatherer society to an agricultural one is described in
"The Development of Agriculture." *National Geographic Education*. Retrieved 8 November, 2023 from https://education.nationalgeographic.org/resource/development-agriculture/

Richard Florida's research is from
Florida, R. (2002). *The Rise of the Creative Class: And How It's Transforming Work, Leisure, Community, and Everyday Life*. Basic Books.

The concept of *Tangping* is described here
"China's new 'tang ping' trend aims to highlight pressures of work culture." *BBC News*.
3 June, 2021. https://www.bbc.com/news/world-asia-china-57348406

The statistics about a disengaged workforce are from
Gallup State of the Global Workplace: 2023 Report.

The story and quote from Larry Gagosian is from
Keefe, P. R. 24 July, 2023. "Larry Gagosian's Expansive Empire." *The New Yorker*.
https://www.newyorker.com/magazine/2023/07/31/larry-gagosian-profile

AnnaLee Saxenian's study is described here
Fox, J. (December, 2014). "What still makes Silicon Valley so special." *Harvard Business Review*.
https://hbr.org/2014/12/what-still-makes-silicon-valley-so-special

The story of Front 242 and Headhunter is from
Festival Forte. (15 June, 2015). "Front 242 // Belpop Documentary 2008 [Video]." *YouTube*.
https://youtu.be/E99NNvo8nW4?si=PjSyvsXOu6flkUdY

The Story of OMD and Atomic Kitten is from
Bagwell, M (January 29, 2021). "'Kraftwerk invented Atomic Kitten': The untold tale of the British girl group's rocky road to a no.1 hit," *Huffington Post*,
https://www.huffingtonpost.co.uk/entry/atomic-kitten-whole-again-kerry-katona-andy-mcclusky-omd_uk_6012b25dc5b6b8719d8a33dc

The Story of Christopher McCandless is told in
Krakauer, J. (1997). *Into The Wild*. Anchor Books.

PART SIX: DARE TO BE TWENTYSOMETHING

The story about Jaqueline Gold is from
"Jacqueline Gold freed women to shamelessly enjoy themselves." *The Economist*,
(23 March, 2023). https://www.economist.com/obituary/2023/03/23/jacqueline-gold-freed-women-to-shamelessly-enjoy-themselves

The Quarter-Life Crisis and the quote about it is from
Zilca, R. (7 March, 2016). "Why your late twenties is the worst time of your life." *Harvard Business Review*. https://hbr.org/2016/03/why-your-late-twenties-is-the-worst-time-of-your-life

The statistics about a mental health crises in your 20s and some of the quotes
are taken from
Witman, P. D. and Rich, D. (2015). "Predictors of the greatest problems facing CIOs:
Hiring IT talent is now number one. *Review of Business Information Systems (RBIS)*,
19(4), 33-40.

The statistics about mental health disorders in 18-24 years olds is from
"Depression Across Age Groups." (n.d.). *Brainsway*.
https://www.brainsway.com/knowledge-center/depression-across-age-groups/

The story of Lena Dunham's pitch and the featured quotes are from
Gillette, F. and Koblin, J. (2022). *It's Not TV: The Spectacular Rise, Revolution, and Future
of HBO*. Viking Books.

The prefrontal cortex and its functions are found here
"Prefrontal cortex." (n.d.). In *ScienceDirect*. Retrieved from
https://www.sciencedirect.com/topics/medicine-and-dentistry/prefrontal-cortex

The study about risk-taking in adolescents is from
Duell, N et al (2017). "Age Patterns in Risk Taking Across the World." *Journal of Youth
Adolescence*, 47(5), 1052-1072. https://pubmed.ncbi.nlm.nih.gov/29047004/

Abraham Lincoln's ugliness including featured quotes is from
Douglas, K. (24 March, 2018). "Was Abraham Lincoln ugly?" *Medium*.
https://medium.com/@nelynyc/was-abraham-lincoln-ugly-fcf9e1ea6f66

Except the quote from the encounter with a woman which is from
"Was Abraham Lincoln really as ugly as everyone says he was?" *Quora*. Retrieved from
https://www.quora.com/Was-Abraham-Lincoln-really-as-ugly-as-everyone-says-he-was

The notes on attractiveness bias are from
Porter-Whistman, J. (24 January, 2022). "Physical attractiveness bias in
hiring." *PerceptionPredict.ai Blog*. https://www.perceptionpredict.ai/blog/
physical-attractiveness-bias-in-hiring

The correlation of height and leadership is from
"Potential leaders: Height helps, but so does being smart. *IdeasForLeaders.com*.
https://ideasforleaders.com/Ideas/potential-leaders-height-helps-but-so-does-being-smart/

The Bob Pittman quote is from
Parrish, S. (Host). (n.d.). "Bob Pittman: Lessons from building media empires
– founder's field guide" (Ep. 12). [Audio podcast episode]. In *Invest Like the
Best*. *Happyscribe*. https://www.happyscribe.com/public/invest-like-the-best/
bob-pittman-lessons-from-building-media-empires-founder-s-field-guide-ep

The idea about pretend adulthood is from
Zilca, R. (7 March, 2016). "Why your late twenties is the worst time of your life." *Harvard Business Review*. https://hbr.org/2016/03/why-your-late-twenties-is-the-worst-time-of-your-life

PART SEVEN: DARE TO GET OLDER

The story about Dietrich Mateschitz is from
Tremayne, D. (22 October, 2022). "Obituary: Remembering Dietrich Mateschitz, Red Bull and AlphaTauri's quiet patriarch." *Formula1.com*. https://www.formula1.com/en/latest/article.obituary-remembering-dietrich-mateschitz-red-bull-and-alphatauris-quiet.7CNRiGEhYVanRPbQAx79y.html

The summary of when we do our greatest work in various fields is from
"At what age do we do our greatest work?" *Things Made Thinkable*. Retrieved from https://www.thingsmadethinkable.com/item/at_what_age_do_we_do_our_greatest_work.php

The section on authors and ageing as well as the direct quote is from
Danenbarger, J. (21 September, 2019). "Is there a right age to be a writer?" *Medium*. https://medium.com/@danenbarger/is-there-a-right-age-to-be-a-writer-8028c0a5b9a6

Vera Wang's, Harland Sanders and Ray Kroc's stories are from their respective Wikipedia pages.

Data on positive risk-taking and middle adulthood is from
Rosenbaum, D., Billinger, M., & Pallesen, J. (2022). Positive and negative risk-taking: Age patterns and relations to domain-specific risk-taking. Personality and individual differences, 188, 111434. DOI:10.1016/j.alcr.2022.100515

The observations about fluid and crystallized intelligence is from
"How we use fluid vs. crystallized intelligence." *Psych Central*. Retrieved from https://psychcentral.com/health/fluid-vs-crystallized-intelligence

The story of August Kekulé and his quote is from
Singer, M. (6 February, 2005). "The misfit." *The New Yorker*. https://www.newyorker.com/magazine/2005/02/14/the-misfit-2

The story of Hans Rosling is from
Roser, M. (14 February, 2017). "Seeing human lives in spreadsheets: The work of Hans Rosling." *The BMJ Opinion*. https://blogs.bmj.com/bmj/2017/02/14/seeing-human-lives-in-spreadsheets-the-work-of-hans-rosling/

The story about George Clooney and Steven Spielberg is from
Parker, I. (14 April, 2008). "Somebody has to be in control." *The New Yorker*. https://www.newyorker.com/magazine/2008/04/14/somebody-has-to-be-in-control

The story and quotes from Adam Mastroianni are taken from
Mastroinni, A. (14 March, 2023). "You can't reach the brain through the ears." *Experimental History*. https://www.experimental-history.com/p/you-cant-reach-the-brain-through

The quote about wisdom is from
Hart, D. B., (2013). *The Experience of God: Being, Consciousness, Bliss.*

The Philip Roth quote is from
Roth, P. (2007). *Everyman*. Vintage, Reprint Edition.

The Happiness Curve research is described here
Haden, J. (30 January, 2020). "Research shows people become increasingly unhappy until age 47.2. Here's how to minimize the negative effect of the 'Happiness Curve.'" *Inc*. https://www.inc.com/jeff-haden/scientists-just-discovered-mid-life-crisis-peaks-at-age-47-heres-how-to-minimize-effect-of-happiness-curve.html

The Orson Welles quote is from
Cousins, M. (Director). (2018). *The Eyes of Orson Welles* [Film]. BofA Productions.

CONCLUSION: BEING THE DIFFERENCE

The story and quote of Nick Cave is from
Cave, N. (10 January, 2023). "I asked ChatGPT to write a song in the style of Nick Cave and this is what it produced. What do you think?" The Red Hand Files.
https://www.theredhandfiles.com/chat-gpt-what-do-you-think/

And
Cave, N. (10 August, 2023). "I Know You've Talked About ChatGPT Before, but What's Wrong with Making Things Faster and Easier?" *The Red Hand Files*.
https://www.theredhandfiles.com/chatgpt-making-things-faster-and-easier/

And
Cain, S. (17 January, 2023). "'This Song Sucks': Nick Cave responds to ChatGPT song written in style of Nick Cave." *The Guardian*.
https://www.theguardian.com/music/2023/jan/17/this-song-sucks-nick-cave-responds-to-chatgpt-song-written-in-style-of-nick-cave

The Rick Rubin quote is from
Rubin, R. (2023). *The Creative Act: A Way of Being*. Penguin Press.

ABOUT THE AUTHOR

MAGNUS LINDKVIST is a trendspotter and futurologist. He calls his work "intellectual acupuncture," aiming to change how we think about the future by provoking us with ideas, enabling new questions and challenging our world view. He lives in Stockholm, Sweden, together with his wife Vesna and two children.

Contact the author for advice, training or speaking opportunities:
www.magnuslindkvist.com

Also by the author:
Everything We Know Is Wrong, 2009
The Attack of the Unexpected, 2010
When the Future Begins, 2013
The Minifesto, 2016
The Future Book, 2023
The Reset Book, 2023

BY THE SAME AUTHOR

£9.99/$12.95
ISBN: 978-1-911687-87-0

HOW TO
BOUNCE BACK
FROM A CRISIS

CONCISE ADVICE

THE
RESET
BOOK

"ANYONE NEEDING TO START AGAIN, CHANGE
COURSE OR RESET SOME PART OF THEIR LIFE,
SHOULD READ THIS BRILLIANT BOOK."
NEIL FRANCIS,
AUTHOR OF *THE CREATIVE THINKING BOOK*
AND *THE ENTREPRENEUR'S BOOK*

MAGNUS LINDKVIST

LID

£9.99/$12.95
ISBN: 978-1-911687-68-9